THE COMPOSITION OF PLATO'S *APOLOGY*

By

R. HACKFORTH, M.A.

*Fellow of Sidney Sussex College
and Lecturer in Classics in the
University of Cambridge*

CAMBRIDGE

AT THE UNIVERSITY PRESS

1933

MGE

PRINTED IN GREAT BRITAIN

PREFACE

The main purpose of this essay is to determine, so far as possible, the relation of the *Apology* of Plato to the actual speech delivered by Socrates at his trial. My justification for this attempt is the wide variation of opinion which at present prevails amongst Platonists and historians of Greek Philosophy. While no one suggests nowadays that we have a verbatim report, we find at one end of the scale a German scholar, E. Horneffer, holding that Plato has given an absolutely true and faithful reproduction of Socrates' own speech; a rather more guarded, but substantially identical position is taken up in this country by the late Professor Burnet in his edition of the *Euthyphro, Apology* and *Crito*, published in 1924, and by Professor A. E. Taylor in *Plato, the Man and his Work*, which appeared in 1926. A middle position is occupied by those who attribute to Plato a certain amount of modification, whether by way of amplification or suppression or shift of emphasis, but no thoroughgoing transformation or absolute invention: the most prominent advocates of this type of view are Ivo Bruns in *Das Literarische Porträt der Griechen* (1896) and U. von Wilamowitz-Möllendorff in his *Platon*, of which the first edition appeared in 1920. The other extreme is represented by M. Schanz, in his edition of the *Apology* (1893), R. von Pöhlmann in *Sokratische Studien* (1906), M. Pohlenz, in *Aus Platos Werdezeit* (1913), and most recently E. Wolff in his essay on the *Apology* in *Neue Philologische Untersuchungen*, vol. vi (1929). These names are of course only a few of those that might be cited, and there are naturally all shades and degrees of opinion on a subject which must necessarily be discussed or noticed by every student of Socrates and Plato.

It is probable that English scholars are for the most part disposed to accept the view of the two great Platonists who have written in our own language: the more so, since Burnet's edition of the *Apology* is by far the best that has appeared in any country. The late Professor Bury, however, writing in the fifth volume of the *Cambridge Ancient History* (1927), leans distinctly to what may be called the left, holding that 'the epilogue' (*i.e.* the third speech) 'is an addition imagined by Plato', and that 'Plato...may have left out parts of the defence and considerably expanded other parts'. His views are stated more fully in the essay on the Trial of Socrates originally published in the *Rationalist Press Annual* (1925), and now fortunately more accessible in his

Selected Essays, posthumously published (1930). The most recent work in English bearing upon the subject is Mr Coleman Phillipson's *Trial of Socrates* (1928), whose judgment substantially coincides with that of Burnet and Taylor. Finally it may be mentioned that Professor Gilbert Murray, writing in 1897, probably under the influence of Schanz, pronounced the work to be definitely fiction: so far as I know he has made no later pronouncement.

I do not claim to have weighed all the arguments put forward by the writers whom I have mentioned: and if I had it would be exceedingly tedious to pass them in review. While I believe that I have taken account of the more important amongst them, I have attempted an independent study of the *Apology*. If my suggestions are in many points opposed to the conclusions of Burnet, I should not be supposed to underrate the debt which I owe to the work of a scholar who has been my chief guide and stimulus since I first began to study Greek Philosophy more than twenty years ago.

My thanks are due to Mr F. H. Sandbach, Fellow of Trinity College, for reading proofs and for a number of helpful criticisms.

R. H.

CAMBRIDGE
November 1932

CHAPTER I

INTRODUCTION

The *Apology* is in form, of course, the report of a speech made on a definite occasion, a speech delivered in the hearing of several hundreds of persons, of whom the reporter was one. Whatever its precise date, no one doubts that, when it appeared, many if not most of those who were present in the court when Socrates spoke could easily remember at least the general outline of his speech. Hence it would seem natural to believe that the report is at least substantially faithful: Plato, it has been said, had to reckon with those who knew the facts, and could not have imposed upon them a fiction: he could not have ventured on anything more than that degree of "literary dressing" or touching up with which we are familiar in such speeches as that of Demosthenes *On the Crown*. Further, the circumstances of the *Apology* differentiate it completely from Plato's dialogues and the Σωκρατικοὶ λόγοι in general, so that even those who believe that the Socrates whom we meet there is often Platonised have no right to apply their views, their prejudices and their arguments here. The very circumstance that Plato, who never appears in the dialogues, has twice (34 A, 38 B) indicated his own presence at the trial, might be thought to put the matter beyond dispute.

This judgment, however, implies one assumption, namely that the *Apology* was certain to be understood by its original readers as claiming to be an authentic report. If it was not, if those into whose hands it came expected to find a fiction, or a mixture of fiction with fact, and if Plato knew that was what they would expect, he would have had no reason to fear their memories. Now I do not think it is possible to prove that this was their expectation: but I would urge that we have as much ground for assuming it as for assuming the opposite. The Greeks of the fifth and fourth centuries had no published official reports of any sort; they had no newspaper reports of proceedings in their law-courts; their conception of an accurate record of an event or a speech is therefore likely to have been far other than that of ourselves who are accustomed to these things, and their demand for and expectation of accuracy is likely to have been far less urgent. Apart from such *a priori* considerations our main guide must be the speeches in Thucydides. The historian has, on his own admission, filled in the gaps in his own memory or that of his informants by inserting what the circumstances of the case would make it

most suitable for his characters to say; and it is
plain that he feels no scruples about doing so,
although his respect for truth and his desire for
accuracy are certainly above the average of ancient
writers. Why did he take this course which appears to us so unnecessary? Why could he not be
content to give his own analysis of a situation
instead of always, or almost always, throwing it
into the form of a speech? Because, I imagine, the
Greeks, or at least the Athenians, preferred and
expected their writers to incorporate a dramatic
element, and because the vividness of impression
thus obtained seemed far more important to them
than accuracy of record.[1] The majority of the
speeches in Thucydides represent his analysis of
a political situation, but there are some which are
really, in whole or in part, sketches of character,
whether national or individual. The clearest examples of the individual character-sketch are contained in the speeches of Pericles (II, 60–4) and
of Alcibiades (VI, 16–18): for here, as has been

[1] Cf. Jebb, 'The Speeches in Thucydides', in *Hel-
lenica*, p. 254: 'The same love of the concrete and
comprehensible which moved the early Greeks to
clothe abstract conceptions of superhuman power in
the forms of men and women...led them also to
represent the energy of the human spirit as much as
possible in the form of speech'.

observed,[1] the two statesmen are represented as claiming for themselves just those qualities which Thucydides himself elsewhere attributes to them.

The fifth century was a stranger to one form of literature, namely the biography or the biographical essay: its substitute was the fictitious or semi-fictitious speech of the historian and the epideictic oration of the Sophist. The want seems to have been recognised in the fourth century: Isocrates writing his *Evagoras* about 370 B.C. claims[2] that he is the first writer to undertake the difficult task of celebrating a man's virtues in prose (ἀνδρὸς ἀρετὴν διὰ λόγων ἐγκωμιάζειν). Xenophon followed his example in his *Agesilaus*, but even in the fourth century it cannot be said that biography established itself as a distinct literary form. A writer who wished to preserve the memory of a distinguished man would naturally, in the first or second decade of the fourth century, turn to the medium of the fictitious speech: and so would a writer who wished to attack the dead. In the case of Socrates we have two examples of this, apart from Plato and Xenophon: the pamphlet written by the Sophist Polycrates (probably about 388) which took the form of a speech by Anytus, one of the actual prosecutors in 399, and the defence written by Lysias, a reply to this,

---

[1] Jebb, *ibid.*, pp. 270–1.　　[2] §§ 8–11.

which took the form of Socrates' own speech in his defence. It is clear that Polycrates gave no indication, by way of preface or incidental comment, that the speech was fictitious: for if he had, it would not have been possible for later antiquity to mistake it[1] for the real speech delivered by Anytus: and it is probable that the same holds good of Lysias' defence. Nobody supposes that either of these speeches adheres closely to the speeches at the trial, and we happen to know that Polycrates alludes to an event of the year 394; on the other hand, it is unlikely that the two writers carefully avoided repeating anything that they knew to have been said at the trial.

These considerations justify us in refusing to follow those who assert that it is *a priori* incredible that Plato, in his *Apology*, can have departed widely from the actual speech delivered by Socrates. No doubt that assertion is better justified the nearer we date the composition of the *Apology* to the trial; hence the importance of attempting, as I shall, to fix that date at least approximately.

In connexion with these preliminary considerations it is convenient to deal with one further

[1] For the evidence see Libanius, ed. R. Foerster, v, pp. 2–3. Foerster is certainly right in thinking that Libanius had the work of Polycrates before him.

point, namely the presence of Plato at the trial, on which much stress has been laid. I do not doubt that Plato was in fact present, and that his mentioning his presence is intentional; but the intention was not, I think, to convince his readers that he was giving them an accurate report of the court proceedings, but rather to suggest that he was intimate enough with Socrates to interpret his life. In both places where his name occurs (34 A and 38 B) special intimacy is suggested. In the former, Plato is one of the young men whose elder relations Socrates challenges Meletus to call as witnesses, and he is perhaps reserved for the last place but one in the list in order to suggest that his admiration for Socrates is fully as great as that of the last to be named, Apollodorus, who, as Burnet reminds us, is 'always represented as one of the most enthusiastic admirers of Socrates'. In the later passage, Plato is the first mentioned of the four friends who offer security for payment of a thirty-minae fine. This is assuredly close to fact: but I do not feel sure that the four persons named, and no others, were actually sitting close together, so that they could concoct the suggestion of a security on the spur of the moment, though of course that is not impossible; it seems more likely that a large number of Socrates' friends, including these four, had agreed earlier to guarantee a sum between them, and that the actual suggestion was made to Socrates at the last moment by Crito, his contemporary and fellow-demesman (33 D). In any case Plato was amongst the guarantors, and may well be forgiven (if forgiveness is needed) for suggesting that he, as a special intimate of Socrates, had been foremost amongst those who had done their utmost to save his life.[1]

[1] In *Phaedo*, 59 B, similarly the intention of the words Πλάτων δ', οἶμαι, ἠσθένει, is to suggest that Plato was one of the 'inner circle'.

CHAPTER II

THE *APOLOGY* OF XENOPHON AND THE DATE OF PLATO'S *APOLOGY*

For determining the fidelity of the *Apology* to the speech actually delivered it would obviously be of great advantage to fix the date of its composition. Unfortunately it is extremely difficult to do this; indeed the views held as to its date have usually been consequent on their authors' views as to its fidelity: the greater the fidelity, the earlier is the date likely to be.

Isocrates, in his *Busiris*, probably composed in or about 388 B.C., implies[1] that a considerable literature had by that date grown up around Socrates. Of this, apart from the work of Plato and Xenophon, there have survived some fairly considerable fragments of the dialogues of Aeschines, and very scanty fragments of Antisthenes.[2] An examination of these fragments throws no light on our question, since no connexion can be

[1] § 6.
[2] Wilamowitz doubts whether Antisthenes wrote any Socratic dialogues; but that he did so is asserted by Panaetius (Diog. Laert. II, 64).

traced between them and the *Apology*. We also
know something of an *Accusation of Socrates* composed by the Sophist Polycrates, the date of which
must lie between 394 and 388; this pamphlet, the
contents of which can be partially reconstructed
from the speech in which Libanius, a rhetor of
the fourth century A.D., attempts to reply to it,
has some bearing on our question, and will be
considered later. Plato's own dialogues are of
little help; it might seem natural, at first sight,
to connect the *Apology* with the dialogues staged
round the trial and death of Socrates, the *Euthyphro*, *Crito* and *Phaedo*: but to realise how delusive
such external connexions are we need only remember the opening sentences of the *Timaeus*, a
dialogue certainly separated by many years from
the *Republic* with which it is there brought into
connexion. With regard to stylometric tests, we
can place only a limited reliance upon these, since
the *Apology* is not a dialogue and can only be
compared with dialogues: but for what they are
worth these tests indicate that the work belongs
to the first of the three groups distinguished by
C. Ritter, and now generally accepted. But this
group contains a large number of dialogues, and
stylometry has not made good any claim to es-
tablish the sequence of these, still less their date;
the latest of them may possibly be as late as

383,[1] and so far as I am aware, no scholar has given any convincing reason why the *Apology* should not be one of the latest, if our judgment be based on the Platonic dialogues alone. Indeed it seems vain to attempt to find any date by this method; and *a priori* it is no more incredible that Plato should have reproduced the scene of the trial sixteen years after its occurrence, than that he should have waited approximately that length of time before describing the last scene in the prison.[2] I do not in fact believe, nor do I think anyone would suggest, that the work was composed so late as this: and no doubt a variety of considerations which make it improbable will suggest themselves to any reader. But it is only when upper and lower limits of date have been fixed on other grounds, and the wide period 399–383, with which we must start, has been considerably narrowed, that we shall be justified in reverting to the relation of the *Apology* to the dialogues.

[1] G. C. Field, *Plato and his Contemporaries*, pp. 72–4, has to my mind successfully defended the traditional explanation of the well-known allusion in *Symp.* 193 A to the διοικισμός of Mantinea.

[2] The *Phaedo* is unquestionably amongst the latest dialogues of the first group: for a recent argument connecting it closely in date with the *Symp.* see L. Robin's recent edition (1929) of the latter dialogue.

Our best hope of determining a *terminus post quem* lies in a consideration of the relation of the work to the *Apologia* which has come down to us with the manuscripts of Xenophon. If it can be proved that this *Apologia*[1] was written before Plato's, and that it is a genuine work of Xenophon, it will follow that PA cannot well be earlier than 394. This inference, if not absolutely certain, will be highly probable: for it was not until 394 that Xenophon returned to Greece from Asia: and it is most unlikely that he became acquainted with any of the Socratic literature, with which he claims acquaintance in § 1, before his return; or that, if he did, he had the leisure or inclination to add to it.[2]

[1] I shall subsequently denote this work by the symbol XA, and the Platonic *Apology* by the symbol PA, when referring to the relation between the two works.

[2] It is possible that Xenophon was in Greece for a few months in 399. Dakyns (*The Works of Xenophon*, I, pp. xcvi–xcvii) thinks it at least improbable that he came back to Athens then. It is in any case highly improbable that he wrote XA at this time, for in that case the death of Anytus, mentioned in § 31, must have occurred almost immediately after that of Socrates; and such swift retribution would surely have found some mention in extant literature; indeed the writer of XA himself could hardly have omitted to make capital of it.

There has been considerable discussion of XA in recent years. Wilamowitz argued in favour of late date and consequent spuriousness in *Hermes*, XXXII (1897): though in his work on Plato (1920) he appears to have modified[1] his earlier judgment to the extent of allowing the Xenophontic authorship to be conceivable. On the linguistic side the most important studies are those of O. Immisch[2] and L. Gautier[3]: the former goes so far as to say that if the work had reached us without its author's name we should certainly have assigned it to Xenophon: the latter in his study of the language of Xenophon, while admitting that the work is too short for linguistic tests to be absolutely cogent, is inclined to accept Immisch's vindication. O. Frick[4] supports Immisch's conclusions by further linguistic points, and also by considerations of a general nature, particularly of the relation of XA to PA and to the *Memorabilia*. The most important work which has appeared since Wilamowitz's article is that of Hans von Arnim,[5] who argues for the authenticity of XA,

[1] *Platon*, II, p. 50.
[2] *Neue Jahrbücher f. d. klass. Altertum*, 1900, pp. 389 ff.
[3] *La Langue de Xénophon*.
[4] *Dissert. Philolog. Halenses*, XIX (1911).
[5] Xenophon's *Memorabilien und Apologie des Sok.* Copenhagen, 1923.

and for the order XA, PA, *Memorabilia*. Later discussions have been published by H. Gomperz[1] and A. Busse,[2] who both accept authenticity, but place XA later than PA. Most recently K. v. Fritz[3] recurs to Wilamowitz's original view, that XA is both spurious and late.

To examine the arguments put forward by these writers, which are numerous and in many cases highly complicated, would be tedious and is, I venture to think, needless. Many of the arguments on both sides seem to me bad, not excepting some of those put forward by von Arnim. Nevertheless there is one argument set by that scholar in the forefront of his book which seems entirely cogent, and which has certainly not been refuted by later writers. It is an argument, not indeed in support of Xenophon's authorship (which the writer tends to assume as a necessary corollary of early date) but in favour of priority of XA to PA. Like most cogent arguments, it is simple: if the author knew PA he could not have asserted, as he does at the outset, that all the previous writers on the subject of Socrates' trial had failed

[1] *Neue Jahrbücher f. d. klass. Altertum*, 1924, pp. 129–173.

[2] 'Xenophon's Schutzschrift und Apologie', *Rhein. Mus.* 79, 3 (1930), pp. 215 ff.

[3] 'Zur Frage der Echtheit der XA', *Rhein. Mus.* 80, 1 (1931), pp. 36–68.

to account for the 'lofty tone' (μεγαληγορία) which he had assumed, with the result that that tone had appeared rather foolish (ἀφρονεστέρα): whereas they should have explained that Socrates thought death preferable to continued life. 'For as to the nature and the motives of this μεγαληγορία the Platonic *Apology* gives far clearer and more satisfactory information than the Xenophontic, and that too in such a way that Xenophon's own object, that of justifying and exalting Socrates, is more completely attained. Who that reads the Platonic *Apology* to-day can fail to understand that the man who defended himself thus did not *expect* to be acquitted, and moreover did not *wish* to be if that were only possible through a sacrifice of his principles? So strongly emphasised is this side of the Socratic defence that one is inclined to conjecture that Plato has exaggerated it in his record, in order to answer completely and once for all the question which Xenophon also raises, viz. "Why did not Socrates defend himself to more purpose"' (*op. cit.* p. 12). And later on (p. 19): 'I regard it as impossible that Xenophon, by way of amplification and correction of the Platonic version known to him, should have put forward another, which...explains the Socratic μεγαληγορία less convincingly from the psychological standpoint, and which makes it appear more open to objection from the ethical'.

The fact that von Arnim is here assuming Xenophon as the author does not detract from the value
of his argument for the priority of XA to PA: it ap-
plies equally well to an unknown author. So far as
I can judge, the reasons which have prevented its
general acceptance, or which have caused it to be
ignored or underrated, are (1) that XA is thought
to contain borrowings from or allusions to PA,
and to the *Phaedo* which is certainly later than
PA, (2) that its author is thought to copy from
the *Memorabilia*, and those parts of the *Memorabilia* which are later than PA, (3) that those who
regard the work as too contemptible for Xenophon to have written are loth to accept an early
date, since the probability of Xenophontic authorship is certainly increased by such acceptance.

I will therefore endeavour briefly to reply to
these three objections:

1. (*a*) *Supposed borrowings from or allusions to PA.*

(i) § 23. κελευόμενος ὑποτιμᾶσθαι οὔτε αὐτὸς
ὑπετιμήσατο οὔτε τοὺς φίλους εἴασεν, ἀλλὰ καὶ
ἔλεγεν ὅτι τὸ ὑποτιμᾶσθαι ὁμολογοῦντος εἴη ἀδικεῖν.
As everyone knows, PA makes Socrates propose
by way of ὑποτίμησις or ἀντιτίμησις first σίτησις
ἐν πρυτανείῳ and then a fine of one mina, raised
on the insistence of his friends to thirty minae.

This would of course be not a case of borrowing, but of deliberate contradiction. The statement of Xenophon (assuming him for convenience, and provisionally, to be the author) is difficult to account for on any hypothesis. But I think it easier to believe him to have said this before reading PA than after reading it. For just as we, when we read in PA the names of those, including Plato himself, who pressed Socrates to make the proposal of a thirty-minae fine and offered to guarantee payment themselves, cannot conceive that Plato is inventing or falsifying, so Xenophon could not have conceived that either. But if he is relying on hearsay or, as is more probable in view of § 1, on other published accounts, his statement may represent an honest belief, *if and only if* those accounts suppressed the fact that Socrates did in the end, with much reluctance, propose a fine. Is it incredible that they did make this suppression? I think not: it is only the honesty of a Plato that admits what, as Burnet rightly says,[1] was not really inconsistent with Socrates' attitude: other apologists of Socrates thought that the proposal of a money fine *was* inconsistent, and therefore suppressed it. I do not argue that they made the positive statement that Socrates refused the suggestion made in court by his

[1] In his note on 38 B 1.

friends: that I take to be Xenophon's own inference
from their silence.[1] In any case it is no more difficult to postulate this suppression in Xenophon's
authorities than to account for Xenophon's own
denial of what was undoubtedly a fact, and what
he must have realised to be a fact after reading
PA.

(ii) § 30. The 'prophecy' here attributed to
Socrates is thought to be based on PA, 39 C. But
there is no great similarity in the language in
which the intention to prophesy is expressed,
while the contents of the two prophecies are entirely different. That dying men prophesy truth
was of course a common Greek belief; and Xenophon, whose faith and interest in μαντική was
especially great, did not need to read Plato to
get the idea of making Socrates prophesy. That
Socrates did prophesy on this occasion was probably either a fact, or a common report[2]: in either
case Plato and Xenophon may quite well have
recorded it independently of one another. There
is just as much, and just as little, reason for saying that Plato's source here is XA.

(iii) § 9 is said to borrow from PA, 38 E. In

[1] For the account of the ἀντιτίμησις in Diogenes
Laertius, II, 41–2, see *infra*, p. 136.

[2] The *motif* is repeated in a different connexion in
Phaedo, 84.

both places Socrates says that he would rather die than save his life by an unworthy appeal to the mercy of his judges.

Here it must be admitted that there is an identity of thought, and a fairly close similarity of language. But these may be explained by supposing that both writers are here faithfully reporting what Socrates did say, and that he said it in the simple straightforward way which they both reproduce. The refusal to plead for mercy was no doubt part of that μεγαληγορία which, as Xenophon tells us, all who had written about Socrates had mentioned. The only word which might perhaps suggest copying is ἀνελευθέρως (ἀνελεύθερον in Plato). The adverb is only here used by Xenophon; but the adjective is used three times (*Mem.* I, 2, 29, III, 10, 5; *Symp.* 8, 23) and seems the natural word here.

(iv) §§ 14–16. The account in XA of the oracle to Chaerephon is said to be an exaggerated version of Plato's: Plato has given[1] the correct form, viz. that 'no one was wiser than Socrates': Xenophon makes the oracle say that 'no one was more generous, just, temperate, or wise'.[2] Now it is

[1] 21 A.

[2] I follow H. Gomperz (*op. cit.* p. 165) in adding ⟨μήτε σοφώτερον⟩ at the end of § 14, in view of σοφὸν δὲ πῶς κτλ. in § 16.

highly probable that Xenophon has exaggerated
what the oracle said; but why should we suppose
that he needed to go to Plato to learn about this
oracle? Is it not probable that he knew about it
before he left Greece in 401? What follower of
Socrates would not have known about it? I may
take this opportunity of adding what appears to
be the explanation of the variation between Plato
and Xenophon on this point. In Xenophon's *Symposium* (IV, 34 ff.) Antisthenes is explaining why,
in spite of his small possessions, he prides himself on his riches: and in §§ 42–3 he says that his
kind of riches (not material, but spiritual) makes
their possessor just and generous: ἀλλὰ μὴν καὶ
πολὺ δικαιοτέρους γε εἰκὸς εἶναι τοὺς εὐτέλειαν
μᾶλλον ἢ πολυχρηματίαν σκοποῦντας. οἷς γὰρ
μάλιστα τὰ παρόντα ἀρκεῖ ἥκιστα τῶν ἀλλοτρίων
ὀρέγονται. ἄξιον δ' ἐννοῆσαι ὡς καὶ ἐλευθερίους
ὁ τοιοῦτος πλοῦτος παρέχεται. Σωκράτης τε γὰρ
οὗτος παρ' οὗ ἐγὼ τοῦτον ἐκτησάμην οὔτ' ἀριθμῷ
οὔτε σταθμῷ ἐπήρκει μοι, ἀλλ' ὁπόσον ἐδυνάμην
φέρεσθαι, τοσοῦτόν μοι παρεδίδου. ἐγὼ δὲ κτλ.
Now it is generally admitted that Xenophon is
in this chapter drawing upon a work (perhaps,
though not necessarily, a dialogue) of Antisthenes
himself; and in the passage just quoted we have
what is quite as much a praise of Socrates as a
self-praise of Antisthenes; particularly in regard

to ἐλευθερία, for it is Socrates, the lavish dis-
penser, not Antisthenes, the recipient, who first
illustrates the quality. This makes it probable
that Xenophon was drawing on some passage in
Antisthenes in which Socrates was credited with
these two qualities, δικαιοσύνη and ἐλευθερία.
Now in XA, § 16, Socrates claims for himself
these same two qualities, and justifies the claim
to the former in words closely resembling those
by which, in the *Symposium* passage, the quality
is claimed for the possessors of spiritual riches:
the sentence in XA is δικαιότερον δὲ τίνα ἂν
εἰκότως νομίσαιτε τοῦ πρὸς τὰ παρόντα συνηρμοσ-
μένου, ὡς τῶν ἀλλοτρίων μηδενὸς προσδεῖσθαι;
the natural inference is that he is drawing upon
the same Antisthenes passage here.[1] If this is
right, then the reason for Xenophon's exag-
geration of the oracle is, not that he believed
himself to be giving a truer version than Plato's
but that he wanted to work into his defence, or

---

[1] The alternative possibility, of self-borrowing, is
unlikely. If the *Apology* is the earlier work, it would
not be natural for Xenophon to turn to it for material
for a speech by Antisthenes. If the *Symposium* is the
earlier, Xenophon would be more likely to have referred to the *direct* praise of Socrates in the work of
Antisthenes, than to the *indirect* praise in his own
Antisthenes-speech.

praise, of Socrates a mention of the virtues, be-
sides that of wisdom, which he had found mentioned previously in Socratic literature.[1] The
fourth quality, σωφροσύνη, which is substantiated
in § 16 by the words τίνα μὲν γὰρ ἐπίστασθε
ἧττον ἐμοῦ δουλεύοντα ταῖς τοῦ σώματος ἐπιθυ-
μίαις; is such an obvious addition to round off the
list that it demands no explanation.

(b) *Supposed borrowing from* Phaedo.

§ 28. Socrates strokes the head of Apollodorus.
This, say Wilamowitz and others, is copied from
Phaedo, 89 B, where he does the same thing to
Phaedo. On this point I have nothing to add to
the remarks of von Arnim (pp. 23–5) and G. C.
Field[2]: and I will not waste space in copying
them out. Burnet remarks that what XA says is
pointless: 'for Apollodorus would hardly wear
his hair long like the youthful Phaedo'; but I do
not know why Xenophon should not make Socrates stroke the head of an intimate friend even
if he did not wear his hair long.

It may well be that scholars have been ready

[1] That there was no real *mala fides* in this re-
handling of the oracle will become apparent when the
general nature and purpose of XA has been explained.
See *infra*, pp. 32 ff.

[2] *Plato and his Contemporaries*, p. 141.

to detect these resemblances between XA and Platonic dialogues partly because Xenophon in his *Symposium* patently imitates and 'improves upon' Plato's dialogue of the same name. But if plagiarism is so patent there, why is it so far from patent here? We should have expected Xenophon (or the author of XA) to have borrowed far more extensively and more grossly from the *Apology* and *Phaedo*. Further, if XA is later than the *Phaedo*, it is *a fortiori* later than the *Gorgias*, for few scholars will contest the priority of the *Gorgias* to the *Phaedo*: and therefore[1] also later than the pamphlet of Polycrates. Is it not then astonishing that no traces have been found either of plagiarism from the *Gorgias*—a dialogue admirably suitable, it would seem, for the pillaging author's purpose—or of concern with the pamphlet, to which Xenophon found it necessary to reply at considerable length in the *Schutz-schrift* (*Mem.* I, 1–2)?

2. *Supposed copying from* Memorabilia.

The question of date and authorship turns largely on this. There are certain sections of XA which correspond, often in the same words

[1] Assuming that the *Gorgias* contains a reply to the pamphlet, as I think is certainly the case. See *infra*, p. 44.

or with very slight modifications, to passages in
Mem. I, 1–2, and IV, 8. Von Arnim has dealt
with the matter exhaustively, arguing that the
Memorabilia version is the later, and that in many
cases the modifications of, the subtractions from,
and the additions to the earlier (XA) version
should be explained as due to the author's having
in the interval become acquainted with PA. The
latter part of this thesis, which had also been
maintained by Frick (though with less detailed
argument), is not, in my judgment, made out;
but that is immaterial to my present inquiry, for
I do not claim to offer any explanation of the
existence of the two versions. On the other hand,
Frick and von Arnim seem to me to have proved
beyond doubt that XA is the earlier version. The
case is particularly clear as regards *Mem.* IV, 8
(a chapter which has sometimes been thought
spurious, in whole or in part, on quite inadequate grounds). Frick (whose work seems to be
unknown to von Arnim) calls attention to certain
minute improvements or corrections made in the
Memorabilia chapter: *e.g.* §4, ἀκούων αὐτοῦ πάντα
μᾶλλον ἢ περὶ τῆς δίκης διαλεγομένου as compared
with XA, § 2, ὁρῶν αὐτὸν περὶ πάντων μᾶλλον
διαλεγόμενον ἢ περὶ τῆς δίκης. But I wish to
refer to another pair of passages, the relation
of which has not, I think, been rightly under-

stood: viz. XA, § 6, and *Mem.* IV, 8, § 8. In
the latter passage Socrates says that if he lives
longer it may be that he will suffer from the
physical and mental infirmities of old age—loss
of sight, hearing, memory, reasoning power etc.,
and become worse than others after having previously been better. And the sentence concludes
thus: ἀλλὰ μὴν ταῦτά γε μὴ αἰσθανομένῳ μὲν
ἀβίωτος ἂν εἴη ὁ βίος, αἰσθανόμενον δὲ πῶς οὐκ
ἀνάγκη χεῖρόν τε καὶ ἀηδέστερον ζῆν; Here the
thought is most curious: why should it have
occurred to Xenophon to raise this antithesis,
to consider the alternatives of (*a*) noticing, and
(*b*) not noticing this failure of physical, mental and
perhaps (if this is implied in the words βελτίων
and χείρω) moral faculties? So impossible does
it seem that anyone should fail to notice the
weakening of his physical powers that von Arnim
feels it necessary to suppose that the ταῦτα, although grammatically it must include these, yet
is intended to refer only to the immediately preceding words καὶ ὧν πρότερον βελτίων ἦν, τούτων
χείρω γίγνεσθαι. This may be right; but it does
little to atone for the unnaturalness of the antithesis. To suppose, with von Arnim, that it is due
to Xenophon's attempt to remould the parallel
passage in XA by an introduction of the idea
expressed in PA, 38 A, ὁ ἀνεξέταστος βίος οὐ βιωτὸς

ἀνθρώπῳ, seems fantastic: the Platonic ἐξέτασις has nothing whatever to do with failing powers of any sort. What has happened, I suggest, is that Xenophon has misunderstood his own previous work. He has taken the words of XA, § 6, ἂν δὲ αἰσθάνωμαι χείρων γιγνόμενος κτλ., as if the emphasis lay on αἰσθάνωμαι rather than on χείρων γιγνόμενος, in other words he has taken them to imply an antithetical protasis ἂν δὲ μὴ αἰσθάνωμαι κτλ.

Has this self-misunderstanding betrayed Xenophon into writing nonsense? I do not think so: he has contrived to work in a genuinely Socratic notion. The state of self-delusion in which a man fancies that he is other than he really is, better (mentally and morally) than he really is, constitutes the fatal 'lie in the soul'.[1] Then in truth life is unliveable. The opposite condition, when he does realise his deterioration, is not so bad: life then is of course 'worse' and more unpleasant than it was, but there is still the possibility of avoiding mistakes by leaning on the judgment of others. Nevertheless, although we can and, I think, should interpret the antithetical clauses in the *Memorabilia* passage in this sense, the unnaturalness of the antithesis still remains; for it is inappropriate, and in fact unmeaning, in connexion with the

[1] Plato, *Rep.* 382 B.

physical weakening which has been made the most prominent kind of weakening of powers mentioned in the preceding sentences. Why is it that Xenophon has imported into the *Memorabilia* passage a consideration of the possibility of *moral* deterioration, which does not figure in the *Apology* passage? This cannot be explained simply by that particular self-misunderstanding which I have already exposed: the probability is that it was reinforced by another: he took χείρων (in ἂν δὲ αἰσθάνωμαι χείρων γιγνόμενος) not in the sense which its preceding context shows that it really bore, *i.e. physically* worse and worse at remembering, but in a *moral* sense; and hence after reproducing the reference to loss of memory he added the words καὶ ὧν πρότερον βελτίων ἦν, τούτων χείρω γίγνεσθαι, thus smoothing the way for the antithesis which follows, and which, as I have said, he supposed to be implicit in his own earlier words.

Hence I submit that, so far from finding in this pair of parallel passages a proof that XA copies from *Memorabilia*, it is impossible to understand the meaning and train of thought in *Memorabilia* except on the reverse hypothesis.

I turn now to the correspondences between XA and *Mem.* I, 1–2 (the *Schutzschrift*) which chapters are commonly, and rightly, regarded as the earliest part of the *Memorabilia*. There is not in this case so much close verbal correspondence as in the case of *Mem.* IV, 8, but there is enough to make it certain that the writer of one has drawn on the other.

It appears to me that the case which has been made for the priority of XA here is, as a whole, less convincing than in the previous instance. In particular von Arnim's main argument has the disadvantage of assuming to start with that Xenophon is the author of XA. If indeed we grant that assumption there is much force in what he says in regard to XA, §§ 11–13. 'If XA is here borrowing from *Memorabilia*, then Xenophon has put into the mouth of Socrates himself his own earlier defence of Socrates: a procedure which would not only put the historical credibility of XA in a very unfavourable light for us, but would certainly have had an astonishing effect upon his contemporaries. For in *Mem.* I, 1, there is nothing to suggest that Xenophon is reproducing Socrates' own defence. On the contrary, the reader cannot help assuming that Xenophon is expressing his own view upon the validity of the accusation brought against Socrates. To come upon these passages again in a later writing, with only slight verbal changes, as the speech made by Socrates himself, would have been bound

to cause surprise to readers in antiquity'
(p. 55).

Everyone who has dealt with the present topic
has remarked the fact that XA uses the word
φωνή in § 12 when speaking of Socrates' δαιμόνιον,
whereas the *Memorabilia* avoids the word. This
contrast has been used by both sides in the con-
troversy, and I shall not attempt to judge between them: not only because I should have
little hope of carrying conviction by means of a
necessarily lengthy examination of the complicated arguments put forward, but also because
I am more than doubtful whether there is really
any difference between the views of the δαιμόνιον
taken in the two works. I have mentioned the
point chiefly because I wish to protest against
the assumption that one version or the other has
necessarily been influenced by PA. In particular
it seems very improbable that the *Memorabilia*
account should be so influenced: why should
Xenophon have gone to PA for information
about a matter with which he must have been
acquainted at first-hand in his personal association with Socrates? And as to XA, assuming
that Xenophon was not its author, why should
his mere use of the word φωνή betray Platonic
influence? It is surely beyond doubt that Plato
could not have made Socrates call the sign a φωνή

unless Socrates did habitually so call it: hence
the author might have got the word from anyone.
I will however go so far as to say that, *if* we were
compelled to think either version dependent on
PA, there would be more justification for pro-
nouncing the *Memorabilia* version dependent, in
spite of the non-occurrence of the actual word
φωνή: for whereas XA gives the impression that
the sign was always imperative (not prohibitive)
—σημαίνουσα ὅτι χρὴ ποιεῖν, the *Memorabilia* is
careful to include that prohibitive function which
in PA is said to be its *only* function (*Mem.* I, 1,
§ 4, οἱ μὲν πλεῖστοί φασιν ὑπό τε τῶν ὀρνίθων...
ἀποτρέπεσθαί τε καὶ προτρέπεσθαι...καὶ πολλοῖς
τῶν συνόντων προηγόρευε τὰ μὲν ποιεῖν, τὰ δὲ μὴ
ποιεῖν, ὡς τοῦ δαιμονίου προσημαίνοντος. PA, 31 D,
ἀεὶ ἀποτρέπει με...προτρέπει δὲ οὐδέποτε).

I would however rest the case for priority of
XA to *Mem.* I, 1–2, on the correspondence between §§ 24–5 and *Mem.* I, 2, §§ 62–3: herein
differing from von Arnim, who holds (p. 66) that
no conclusion can be drawn from this. My view
of the relation between these passages is partly
taken from Frick (p. 50), but I think I am able to
strengthen his argument.

It will be convenient here to set down the
relevant parts of the two passages:

XA, § 24. ἐμοὶ δὲ τί προσήκει νῦν μεῖον φρονεῖν

ἢ πρὶν κατακριθῆναι, μηδὲν ἐλεγχθέντι ὡς πεποίηκά
τι ὧν ἐγράψαντό με; οὔτε γὰρ ἔγωγε ἀντὶ Διὸς καὶ
Ἥρας καὶ τῶν σὺν τούτοις θεῶν οὔτε θύων τισὶ
καινοῖς δαίμοσιν οὔτε ὀμνὺς οὔτε νομίζων ἄλλους
θεοὺς ἀναπέφηνα. § 25. τούς γε μὴν νέους πῶς ἂν
διαφθείροιμι, καρτερίαν καὶ εὐτέλειαν προσεθίζων;
ἐφ᾽ οἷς γε μὴν ἔργοις κεῖται θάνατος ἢ ζημία,
ἱεροσυλίᾳ, τοιχωρυχίᾳ, ἀνδραποδίσει, πόλεως προ-
δοσίᾳ, οὐδ᾽ αὐτοὶ οἱ ἀντίδικοι τούτων πρᾶξαί τι
κατ᾽ ἐμοῦ φασιν. ὥστε θαυμαστὸν ἔμοιγε δοκεῖ
εἶναι ὅπως ποτὲ ἐφάνη ὑμῖν τοῦ θανάτου ἔργον
ἄξιον ἐμοὶ εἰργασμένον. ἀλλ᾽ οὐδὲ μέντοι ὅτι ἀδίκως
ἀποθνήσκω διὰ τοῦτο μεῖον φρονητέον· οὐ γὰρ
ἐμοὶ ἀλλὰ τοῖς καταγνοῦσι τοῦτο αἰσχρόν ἐστι.

Mem. I, 2, § 62. ἐμοὶ μὲν δὴ Σωκράτης τοιοῦτος
ὢν ἐδόκει τιμῆς ἄξιος εἶναι τῇ πόλει μᾶλλον ἢ
θανάτου. καὶ κατὰ τοὺς νόμους δὲ σκοπῶν ἄν τις
τοῦθ᾽ εὕροι. κατὰ γὰρ τοὺς νόμους, ἐάν τις φανερὸς
γένηται κλέπτων ἢ λωποδυτῶν ἢ βαλλαντιοτομῶν
ἢ τοιχωρυχῶν ἢ ἀνδραποδιζόμενος ἢ ἱεροσυλῶν,
τούτοις θάνατός ἐστιν ἡ ζημία · ὧν ἐκεῖνος πάντων
ἀνθρώπων πλεῖστον ἀπεῖχεν. § 63. ἀλλὰ μὴν τῇ
πόλει γε οὔτε πολέμου κακῶς συμβάντος οὔτε
στάσεως οὔτε προδοσίας οὔτε ἄλλου κακοῦ οὐδενὸς
πώποτε αἴτιος ἐγένετο.... § 64. πῶς οὖν ἂν ἔνοχος
εἴη τῇ γραφῇ; ὃς ἀντὶ μὲν τοῦ μὴ νομίζειν θεούς...
ἀντὶ δὲ τοῦ διαφθείρειν τοὺς νέους κτλ. ...ταῦτα δὲ
πράττων πῶς οὐ μεγάλης ἄξιος ἦν τιμῆς τῇ πόλει;

The reference to capital crimes other than those mentioned in the indictment is relevant and natural in XA,[1] but not in *Memorabilia*. In the former work Socrates is arguing that he has no cause to feel humiliated owing to his condemnation since (*a*) he is innocent of the charges actually brought against him, and (*b*) other crimes punishable by death his accusers have not ventured to charge him with. The reference in (*b*) is relevant in the sense that Socrates is justifying his attitude by his consciousness that he has done nothing, *even apart from the actual charges*, that deserves the death-penalty. In the *Memorabilia*, however, where Xenophon's sole purpose is to rebut the actual charges (whether of Meletus and Anytus, or of Polycrates), the introduction of the crimes catalogued in §§ 62–3 is quite irrelevant; moreover it has all the appearance of an afterthought, and an unhappy one: for the first sentence of § 62, ἐμοὶ μὲν δὴ Σωκράτης τοιοῦτος ὢν ἐδόκει τιμῆς ἄξιος εἶναι τῇ πόλει μᾶλλον ἢ θανάτου, is the natural conclusion[2] of these first two chapters. It is weak and unnatural to follow it up by remarking that Socrates was not a commonplace criminal, a pickpocket, burglar, etc.

[1] Natural, that is, from the writer's standpoint. I do not imply that I think Socrates likely to have spoken thus.   [2] See Additional Note 2, p. 172.

And after he has finished his catalogue Xenophon
has to work his way back again, in § 64, so as
to be able to conclude his chapter with a repetition,
almost verbally identical, of the thought which
had already expressed his conclusion at the
beginning of § 62: ταῦτα δὲ πράττων πῶς οὐ
μεγάλης ἄξιος ἦν τιμῆς τῇ πόλει; It seems to
me that there can be no doubt that XA is here
the original, *Memorabilia* the copy. If XA did
not exist one would want to know why Xenophon
dragged in these §§ 62 and 63 which necessitate
a double ending to the *Schutzschrift*.

(3) Finally I turn to the third of the apparent
reasons why von Arnim's main argument for
the priority of XA to PA has been resisted or
ignored. To assign such an early date to XA
destroys many, and weakens almost all, of the
arguments against Xenophontic authorship: and
many scholars have felt that the work is unworthy of Xenophon.

This feeling can only be met by an examination of its general nature and purpose. As to
these, I cannot accept von Arnim's position. I
see no reason to doubt that the *Apology* is a Σωκρατικὸς λόγος in the ordinary sense, as indeed are
all the Socratic writings of Xenophon. Here, as in
the *Memorabilia Symposium* and *Œconomicus*, he
aims at presenting not an accurate record of fact,

but a picture of Socrates' character as he knew it from his own experience, and from conversation with those who had known him. It is a mistake to claim a historical value for the *Memorabilia* and *Apology*, as von Arnim does, simply on the ground that the author purports to be recording real conversations remembered by himself or communicated to him by others, whereas in the Σωκρατικὸς λόγος (of which Plato's dialogues are of course almost the only extant example) the author takes no responsibility for the truth of what is said. As regards the *Memorabilia*, it misrepresents the case to say that Xenophon takes this responsibility. At the beginning of I, 3, that is to say immediately after the so-called *Schutzschrift*, which is doubtless (as it claims to be) Xenophon's own attempt to defend Socrates against the charges of Meletus and of Polycrates, he says ὡς δὲ δὴ καὶ ὠφελεῖν ἐδόκει μοι τοὺς συνόντας τὰ μὲν ἔργῳ δεικνύων ἑαυτὸν οἷος ἦν, τὰ δὲ καὶ διαλεγόμενος, τούτων δὴ γράψω ὁπόσα ἂν διαμνημονεύσω. Probably his intention, when writing these words, was to confine himself to what he did actually remember of Socrates' acts and words. Hence the first conversation is one between Socrates and Xenophon himself, in the presence of Critobulus; the second is a conversation between Socrates and Aristodemus, which

Xenophon says he heard. But the next three conversations (I, 6), with Antiphon, are recorded without any mention of the means whereby Xenophon came to know about them,[1] and the same is true of the great majority of the dialogues in the following books. According to Field's reckoning, out of about forty conversations thirty make no sort of claim to be reminiscences. Nor does Xenophon anywhere, except in the case of Hermogenes, say that Socrates' interlocutor gave him the substance of the conversation. Hence I can see no grounds for accepting what Field calls 'the simple and natural supposition...that he collected his material in the same manner as he would collect material for his history'.[2] If he had gone about his work on Socrates in the spirit and with the methods of a conscientious biographer or historian, how can we explain the very first words of the *Memorabilia*, πολλάκις ἐθαύμασα κτλ., 'I have often wondered by what arguments those who indicted Socrates persuaded the Athen-

---

[1] Except that at the *end* of the second conversation (I, 6, § 14) he says ἐμοὶ μὲν δὴ ταῦτα ἀκούοντι ἐδόκει κτλ. The position of this remark, together with its absence from the other two conversations, is a pretty clear indication that the 'hearing' is not to be taken seriously.

[2] G. C. Field, *Plato and his Contemporaries,* p. 140.

ians that he was worthy of death.' Why did he not apply to those persons whom he considered best able to tell the truth about it? No, the method of Xenophon in the *Memorabilia* is to trust to memory supplemented by conjecture and invention; he remembers what Socrates was like in general, and the sort of things he used to say, and he composes the dialogues to illustrate Socrates' character and teaching. I do not deny the *possibility* that in some cases the interlocutor named may have supplied some material; but there is no more (if no less) probability of this than in the case of Plato's dialogues. The difference between an early Platonic dialogue and the dialogues in the *Memorabilia* is that Xenophon encloses his dialogues in a framework of personal explanation and comment, while Plato does not. Xenophon's method is to say, *e.g.*, 'I will now write a dialogue showing what Socrates thought about Piety', and then to write it; Plato, an immeasurably greater artist, leaves out the preface (or, it may be, the conclusion) and writes the *Euthyphro*. But the difference is one of form, not of spirit or purpose.[1]

[1] It is irrelevant to this comparison that Plato afterwards—perhaps even from the first—used the Σωκρατικὸς λόγος to express his own philosophical beliefs.

It may be urged, however, that there are at least some conversations which Xenophon expressly attests, apart from the general introductory formula of ɪ, 3, and that one of these is the dialogue with Hermogenes at ɪv, 8, which is, as we have seen, largely a reproduction of what Hermogenes is reported in the *Apology* as having related to Xenophon. Is not this a good ground for regarding the *Apology*, or at least the bulk of if (§§ 1–27), as a genuine historical record?

There are several reasons against taking this view.

(1) Both the *Symposium* and the *Œconomicus* open in the same way. Xenophon 'heard' the whole dialogue *Œconomicus* or the substance of it (ἤκουσα δέ ποτε αὐτοῦ καὶ περὶ οἰκονομίας τοιάδε διαλεγομένου), and 'was present' (παραγενόμενος) at the scene of the *Symposium*. Nobody can take these statements seriously, and in the case of the *Symposium* at least Xenophon cannot have intended them to be taken seriously, for he takes no part in the proceedings and indeed can only have been a child at the date in question.

(2) The latter part of the Hermogenes dialogue (*Mem.* ɪv, 8, §§ 9–10) appears in a substantially identical form in *Apology*, § 26, as what Socrates said to the court after sentence had been

pronounced. If *Memorabilia* is copying from *Apology* (as I believe), the inclusion of these sentences in the conversation of Socrates with Hermogenes is either a deliberate fiction or (as I think more likely) an oversight, due to the fact that Xenophon, when copying, did not notice that in his original they were addressed to the court.

(3) The Hermogenes dialogue is followed in *Mem.* IV, 8, § 10, by the words τοιαῦτα μὲν πρὸς Ἑρμογένην τε διελέχθη καὶ πρὸς τοὺς ἄλλους. Now since such formulae are constantly inserted at the end of dialogues (*e.g.* I, 4, § 19, I, 5, § 6, IV, 3, § 18, IV, 4, § 25), τοιαῦτα must refer to the last conversation alone, and the effect of adding καὶ πρὸς τοὺς ἄλλους is to show that Xenophon was indifferent whether Hermogenes or somebody else was the interlocutor: or, in other words, that he did not intend the ascription in IV, 8, § 4, λέξω δὲ καὶ ἃ Ἑρμογένους τοῦ Ἱππονίκου ἤκουσα περὶ αὐτοῦ, to be taken seriously.

About three-quarters of the *Apology* is in reported speech, resting on the authority of Hermogenes: not only the dialogue between Socrates and Hermogenes before the trial (§§ 3–9) but the actual defence of Socrates before the court (§§ 10–21), the address to the judges after the sentence (§§ 24–6) and the address of consolation

spoken to his friends on leaving the court (§ 27).
We shall be justified in regarding all this as the
author's own invention: for the dialogue is on
the same footing as the dialogues in the *Memorabilia*, and the two addresses do not claim any
different authority from that claimed for the dialogue. But in terming this 'invention' I do not
mean to deny that it includes elements of fact, or
at least of what the author believed to be fact: I
only mean that the composition is of that type
where the primary aim is not to record facts but
to describe a character, or rather certain aspects
of a character. That Xenophon should choose to
describe Socrates' character through the medium
of Socrates' own words was due partly to the
already established literary form of the Σωκρατικὸς
λόγος, partly to the instinctive tendency of his
age to dramatise: we may compare the last
speech of Pericles in Thucydides, II, 62. The disadvantage of this method is that a writer who
lacks experience is liable to put into his subject's
mouth words which he is unlikely to have used,
either on any occasion or at least on the occasion
in question. When Xenophon in his later years
came to write the *Symposium* he shows some consciousness of this danger: for in two places he
feels that he is making Socrates speak in a more
serious or exalted vein than the occasion war-

rants,[1] and makes him apologise accordingly
(VIII, 24, 41).

The worst example of this fault in the *Apology*
is in §§ 16–18, when the author, after expanding
the reply of the Delphic oracle from the motive
which I have already explained, proceeds to make
Socrates substantiate its pronouncements at considerable length. It is perfectly true that Socrates
here becomes 'insufferably arrogant' as Burnet
has said; and it is probably this passage, as much
as any other, that has disposed scholars to doubt
the Xenophontic authorship of the work; Socrates,
they feel, cannot have talked like this, and Xenophon could not have thought he did. The reply is
that Xenophon did not think so. Nor again did
Xenophon suppose that Socrates told Hermogenes that the reason why he had prepared no
defence was because, at his advanced age, death
was preferable to continued life: that reason is,

[1] Incidentally I cannot see that we are warranted
in disconnecting the *Symposium* from the *Memorabilia* and *Apology* in its attitude to Socrates. The dis-
course of Socrates in chapter 8 is, as Dakyns remarks,
an expansion of *Mem.* IV, 1, §§ 1–2, καὶ γὰρ παίζων
οὐδὲν ἧττον ἢ σπουδάζων ἐλυσιτέλει τοῖς συνδιατρίβουσιν.
πολλάκις γὰρ ἔφη μὲν ἄν τινος ἐρᾶν, φανερὸς δ' ἦν οὐ τῶν
τὰ σώματα πρὸς ὥραν, ἀλλὰ τῶν τὰς ψυχὰς πρὸς ἀρετὴν
εὖ πεφυκότων ἐφιέμενος.

of course, Xenophon's own invention. It is, no doubt, untrue, though not, I think, wholly absurd: it may well have been the case that Socrates did feel some weakening of his powers at the age of 70; and when Burnet says 'it would be easy to show that...there was no reason why Socrates should not have looked forward to at least another ten years of activity', he seems to forget that even Plato, whose explanation of Socrates' readiness to die is wholly different from Xenophon's, makes him say, after the sentence, 'If you had waited a little, this would have happened without your intervention; for you see that I am well advanced in years, and near to death'. Still Xenophon's invented reason is, I repeat, untrue: for it disregards the real explanation why Socrates was ready to die, namely his recognition that he could only be acquitted if he agreed to surrender his principles, and substitutes a merely secondary consideration. Why did Xenophon make this substitution? It may be that his insight into the character of Socrates was too shallow to see the truth of the matter; but I should prefer a different explanation. In writing the *Apology* Xenophon had two ends in view: one is the end common to all his Socratic writings, to illustrate Socrates' character by his acts and words; the other is to answer the question 'Why did the gods allow such a righteous man to be put to death'? The answer that he found was that death was really no misfortune for Socrates; his best days were past. ἐμοὶ μὲν οὖν δοκεῖ θεοφιλοῦς μοίρας τετυχηκέναι· τοῦ μὲν γὰρ βίου τὸ χαλεπώτατον ἀπέλιπε, τῶν δὲ θανάτων τοῦ ῥᾴστου ἔτυχεν. Thus does Xenophon (§ 32) begin his closing comment on the death of Socrates: and we could hardly wish for a clearer indication that the explanation which his Socrates has given to Hermogenes of the μεγαληγορία of his address to the judges is simply a projection of Xenophon's own ideas. The other motive, less prominent perhaps but not less real, is revealed not only in the last two sections (§§ 33–4), especially § 34, ἐγὼ μὲν δὴ κατανοῶν τοῦ ἀνδρὸς τήν τε σοφίαν καὶ τὴν γενναιότητα οὔτε μὴ μεμνῆσθαι δύναμαι αὐτοῦ οὔτε μεμνημένος μὴ οὐκ ἐπαινεῖν, but also in § 22, ἀλλ' ἐγὼ οὐ τὰ πάντα εἰπεῖν τὰ ἐκ τῆς δίκης ἐσπούδασα, ἀλλ' ἤρκεσέ μοι δηλῶσαι ὅτι Σωκράτης τὸ μὲν μήτε περὶ θεοὺς ἀσέβης[1] μήτε περὶ ἀνθρώπους ἄδικος φανῆναι περὶ παντὸς ἐποιεῖτο. Moreover the words which immediately follow in § 23 bring the second motive into close connexion with the first: τὸ δὲ μὴ ἀποθανεῖν οὐκ ᾤετο λιπαρητέον εἶναι, ἀλλὰ καὶ καιρὸν ἤδη ἐνόμιζεν ἑαυτῷ τελευτᾶν.

If we interpret the *Apology* in this way I see no

[1] The MSS. have ἀσεβῆσαι, no doubt owing to the following φανῆναι; but the adjective is plainly required by the sense.

reason for doubting that it is an early work[1] of Xenophon's; we know that Xenophon did write an *Apology of Socrates*, on the authority of Demetrius of Magnesia[2] quoted by Diogenes Laertius: nor does there appear to have been any doubt of its genuineness in antiquity.[3]

I need only add a few words regarding the so-called 'Anytus-episode' in §§ 29–31. The anecdote, not given as part of the information supplied by Hermogenes but introduced by a mere λέγεται, is to the following effect. Socrates remarks that Anytus' reason for bringing him to trial is that he had once dissuaded him from bringing up his son to follow his father's trade of a tanner; but Anytus has little reason to pride himself on securing a conviction. Moreover Socrates will venture to prophesy that Anytus' son will not stick at his 'slavish' trade, but will come to a bad

[1] See Additional Note 3, p. 173.

[2] This authority seems implied in the author's statement (II, 57) that Demetrius rejected the Ἀθηναίων Πολιτεία.

[3] The earliest citation of our XA is probably to be found in Athenaeus, 218 E, if Wilamowitz is right in holding that Athenaeus' source in this passage is Herodicus of Babylon (ὁ Κρατήτειος). Herodicus' date is doubtful, but he is certainly not later than the first half of 1st century B.C. and may be as early as 2nd century B.C.

end owing to the lack of proper parental super-
vision. Xenophon appends the remark that this
prophecy was fulfilled, and that Anytus, though
now dead, still bears an evil reputation 'owing
to the bad education he gave his son and his own
lack of decent feeling'.[1]

Much labour has been wasted on arguing that
Socrates is unlikely to have said anything of the
kind. Of course he did not, but the anecdote,[2]
which had come to Xenophon's ears, served well
enough to point Xenophon's moral and adorn his
tale. Anytus' seeming triumph was turned to
disgrace, Socrates' seeming defeat to victory.
We need not suppose that Xenophon believed
the story, still less need we laboriously point out,
e.g., that it is not like Socrates to sneer at Anytus'
trade as δουλοπρεπὴς διατριβή; it would be more
to the point to remember that the Socrates of the
Œconomicus[3] goes out of his way to indulge in a
tirade against base mechanic arts.

---

[1] The statement is confirmed by *Meno*, 95 A, ἀλλ'
οὗτος μὲν ἐάν ποτε γνῷ οἷόν ἐστι τὸ κακῶς λέγειν, παύσεται
χαλεπαίνων, νῦν δὲ ἀγνοεῖ, where Socrates counters
Anytus' prophecy against him.

[2] Possibly, as Dittmar suggests (*Aischines von
Sphettos*, p. 96) it had been already thrown into the
form of a dialogue by Antisthenes.

[3] IV, 2.

We arrive then at 394 as a *terminus post quem*
for the date of Plato's *Apology*. How soon after
that date we must put it cannot be exactly determined. There is nothing to suggest that its
motive, or one of its motives, was to correct
Xenophon.[1] There is a probability, indeed, that
it appeared earlier than the pamphlet directed
against Socrates by the Sophist Polycrates: and
it has often been said that this pamphlet, which
referred to the rebuilding of the Long Walls of
Athens by Conon in 394, must have been composed soon after that event: this inference is
groundless. It is however usually believed that
the *Gorgias* is, *inter alia*, a reply to Polycrates:
this view has recently been ably defended by
J. Geffcken[2] against the reverse view, propounded
by Wilamowitz, that the *Gorgias* provoked Polycrates' pamphlet. The same writer adduces a
number of considerations which all point to the
Gorgias having been composed shortly after

[1] There is an ancient tradition that Plato and
Xenophon were enemies, or literary rivals; it may be
true, though the evidence on which it is based in the
accounts of Aulus Gellius (XIV, 3), Athenaeus (XI,
504), and Diogenes Laertius (III, 34) is far from
strong. The last-named writer makes Plato dislike
too many people—Antisthenes, Aristippus, Aeschines,
Molon, as well as Xenophon.

[2] *Hermes*, 65, 1 (1930).

Plato's return from Sicily in 387 or 386, and consequently to the pamphlet having appeared about, or shortly before, that date.

The reason put forward by Gomperz[1] for holding that PA precedes the pamphlet is that Plato would not have been likely to ignore the specific instances of corruption of the young which the latter alleged. This is not, I think, a very convincing reason, for Plato might have ignored the points made by Polycrates just as easily as he in fact ignores the points made by Meletus and Anytus. Nevertheless it does seem unlikely that Plato, if he thought the attack of Polycrates ought to be answered (as he seems to think in the *Gorgias*), should, before answering it, have composed a defence of Socrates which ignores it. I think, therefore, that Gomperz's argument may be accepted if we restate it in such a way as to take account, not only of Plato's *Apology* and Polycrates' κατηγορία, but of the *Gorgias* as well. This gives us 394 and 387 as *termini*. Any closer approximation it is, in my judgment, impossible to give with any confidence. Geffcken, indeed, suggests that Polycrates was making a sort of reply to the reference of the *Apology* to Socrates' activity as being of a purely private character; but I cannot see any good evidence for this. I would only say that I am inclined to

[1] *Loc. cit.* p. 170.

suggest a date nearer to 394 than to 387, partly
because I do not see why Plato should have held
his hand unduly long, partly because I believe
that during these years Plato's own philosophical
beliefs were beginning to take shape, and his interest gradually turning from the personality of
Socrates to the implication of his teaching; therefore it seems likely that the non-philosophical[1]
Apology should come early, rather than late, in this
period. But such arguments are extremely hazar-
dous, and I am far from wishing to press them.

[1] That the *Apology* is non-philosophical in the
sense that Plato is concerned not to discuss im-
personal philosophical problems but to present an
individual portrait of a philosopher, seems to me
beyond question. I cannot agree with the general
interpretation of Friedländer (*Platon*, ii, pp. 687 ff.),
who finds in it a study of the 'Unity of the Virtues'.
('Die Einheit der Tugenden, die immer wieder in ihr
anklingt, ist beherrschendes Thema vom *Protagoras*
und der aporetischen Definitionsdialogen bis in die
Politeia hinein. Irgendwo auf dieser Zeitlinie muss
die *Apologie* anzusiedeln sein, vielleicht nach dem
Euthyphro'.) Nevertheless it remains true that the
work has an element of φιλόσοφος θεωρία, as Pseudo-
Dionysius *Ars Rhetorica*, viii, 8, well says: for it is, in
his words, παράγγελμα ὁποῖον εἶναι δεῖ τὸν φιλόσοφον.
To show what Socrates was is to show what the true
philosopher ought to be.

CHAPTER III

THE MOTIVE OF PLATO'S *APOLOGY*

The first motive for the composition of the *Apology* that occurs to one as possible is that Plato, having been deeply stirred by Socrates' speech, having seen in it a splendid picture of a life spent in the service of God and of man, felt that it should be preserved to posterity. This, I imagine, is the motive that would generally be accepted by those who believe the work to be a substantial reproduction.[1] But is it applicable to the date we have arrived at? Granting that Plato's memory may have been strong enough to preserve the substance of the speech, would he still have felt the same impulse to preserve it? The answer to this question depends, I think, on the state of Athenian opinion at the time. If Athens had forgotten about Socrates, or lost interest in his fate, we might perhaps say yes: but if his followers had been writing about him, claiming or hinting that he had been unjustly executed, contrasting his noble death with the dishonoured death of his accuser Anytus: if, in

[1] Cf. Horneffer, *Der junge Platon*, p. 132, 'Eine derartige Rede niederzuschreiben, entfliesst aus einem leidenschaftlichen Bedürfnis'.

short, an atmosphere had been created in which the treatment of Socrates in 399 was a subject of eager discussion, and opinion was turning in his favour, is it not probable that a different motive would have determined Plato to write? Would he not, in these circumstances, feel a desire to do all that he could to encourage this turning of public opinion? Would he not feel that his literary genius could and should be employed to this end? On the other hand, if the circumstances were what we have supposed, would not a mere reproduction of Socrates' actual speech have fallen flat? What was needed was not that, the defence that had failed, but a better defence, which he might have made, and which now might be made for him.[1]

[1] Valgimigli (Platone, *Apologia di Socrate*, 1929), who dates the *Apology* soon after Plato's return to Athens (which was not earlier, he thinks, than 396), has realised that the condition of public opinion has an important bearing on its composition. His able reconstruction of the situation on pp. 45–6 seems to me, however, unnecessarily to restrict the scope of current discussion to the topic of Socrates' μεγαληγορία at the trial: I think it more likely that the wider question of the justice of the prosecution and verdict was the main topic. But in any case I agree that 'Pensare a una reproduzione più o meno meccanica della difesa di Socrate non è licito nè possibile ora, per nessun modo'.

The anecdotes in late authors, such as Diodorus (xiv, 37) and Diogenes Laertius (ii, 43) which tell of the repentance of the Athenians for Socrates' execution, and the punishment of his accusers, are no doubt worthless. Modern scholars,[1] however, have often suggested that the trial and its sequel became a topic of keen discussion, and E. Horneffer has called attention to a passage of the *Crito* (48 c) as suggesting some such revulsion of feeling at Athens as I have supposed. Socrates there says that the considerations which Crito has put forward to induce him to escape from prison are such as would weigh with 'the many who lightly put men to death and would bring them to life again, if they could' (μὴ ὡς ἀληθῶς ταῦτα σκέμματα ἦ τῶν ῥᾳδίως ἀποκτεινύντων καὶ ἀναβιωσκομένων γ' ἄν, εἰ οἷοί τ' ἦσαν, οὐδενὶ ξὺν νῷ, τούτων τῶν πολλῶν). The *Crito* can hardly be far removed in date from the *Apology*, and unless 'the many' did regret the execution of Socrates it is difficult to see any point in these words.

[1] *E.g.* C. Ritter, *Platon*, i, p. 77, 'Es heisst in verschiedenen Berichten, die Athenen hätten bald die Verurteilung des Sok. bereut. Nun ja. Es reute sie ja so vieles was sie taten, wie es bei einer durch Majoritätsbeschluss entscheidenden vielköpfigen Menge nicht anders erwartet werden kann'.

It is perhaps possible to find confirmation of this in the *Apology* itself. At 24 A, when Socrates has finished his reply to his 'first accusers' and explained the origin of the long-standing misrepresentation (διαβολή) to which he was exposed, he says, καίτοι οἶδα σχεδὸν ὅτι αὐτοῖς τούτοις ἀπεχθάνομαι, ὃ καὶ τεκμήριον ὅτι ἀληθῆ λέγω καὶ ὅτι αὕτη ἐστὶν ἡ διαβολὴ ἡ ἐμὴ καὶ τὰ αἴτια ταῦτά ἐστιν. καὶ ἐάντε νῦν ἐάντε αὖθις ζητήσητε ταῦτα, οὕτως εὑρήσετε. It seems not improbable that the reference in this last sentence to a later enquiry into Socrates' case reflects the state of affairs at the time that Plato was writing.

Is it possible to conjecture what sort of 'improvement' or reinforcement of the actual defence, which he had heard, would suggest itself to Plato under these circumstances and at this date? To some extent I think it is. He would wish to preserve at least the most important points which he remembered: for that Socrates made an impressive speech is sufficiently indicated by the large minority that voted for his acquittal; at the same time he might well be ready to omit, or abbreviate, points which were no longer matter of dispute. But his principal object would be to incorporate a general interpretation of Socrates' life and personality, and particularly of his services to Athens. I shall attempt to show that this interpretation, which borders upon undisguised encomium, is for the most part concentrated in one section of the *Apology* which is clearly marked off from the rest, and which presents a number of curious points of connexion with what precedes it. This sort of addition was probably more than usually needed in the present case: most contemporary Athenians would not have shrunk from self-laudation and lengthy enumeration of patriotic services. But everything[1] we know of Socrates, apart from the *Apology*, suggests that he would have contented himself with giving a modest and unimpassioned account of his actions, a plain direct refutation of the charges brought against him and an explanation of their underlying ground: which indeed is just what he does in the opening pages of the speech, those pages namely in which I believe Plato to have reproduced the real speech with considerable fidelity.

It is possible that Plato's procedure was partly

[1] Except his claim in the *Gorgias* to be the one true statesman in Athens (521 D ff.). But this exception proves the rule: for this part of the *Gorgias* is Plato's defence, through Socrates' own mouth, against the attack of Polycrates, just as the section of the *Apology* here referred to is his defence against the attack of Meletus and Anytus.

conditioned by what he had himself written previously, namely in the *Euthyphro*. Ritter, following Zeller, believes this short dialogue to
have been composed between the announcement
of the prosecution and the trial: it is argued that
the light, satirical tone in which Socrates' approaching trial is treated could not have been
employed by Plato after the sentence.[1] At 3 A
Euthyphro asks Socrates in what way his accusers charge him with corrupting the young,
and Socrates replies that it is by 'making new
gods and not believing in the old ones'; that is
to say, whereas the actual indictment, as preserved by Xenophon and Diogenes Laertius, formulated two separate counts,[2] that of irreligion
and that of corrupting the young, Socrates here
represents them as really one, of which the first
part merely explains the second. The same procedure is adopted at *Apology*, 26 B, in the dia-

[1] So far as I know, attention has not been drawn
to the closing words of the dialogue, ἐνδειξάμενος
ἐκείνῳ ὅτι...καὶ τὸν ἄλλον βίον ὅτι ἄμεινον βιωσοίμην.
This reference to the 'rest of Socrates' life' could
scarcely have been put into his mouth after the tragic
sequel. Probably Plato, like everyone else, thought
that Socrates would go into exile.

[2] ἀδικεῖ δὲ καὶ τοὺς νέους διαφθείρων, Diog. Laert. II,
40. On this point see *infra*, p. 105.

logue with Meletus, a dialogue the substance of which can hardly, as I shall argue, be true to fact. It may well be that in composing this part of the *Apology* Plato referred to the text of his *Euthyphro*, just as when composing the *Meno* it seems certain that he referred to the text of the *Apology*.[1]

If Plato did write some of his dialogues before writing the *Apology*, the *Euthyphro* is likely to have been one of them. The supposition that he did so gives at least a partial explanation of the dialogue with Meletus, which calls for separate examination, and of the rather curious little dialogue with Callias (20 A–B); Plato, I suggest, had got into the way of thinking of Socrates as normally expressing himself in dialogue: it is only on that supposition that I can account for the curious words at 37 A, where Socrates explains his failure to convince the jury as due to the brief time that he has *conversed* with them: πέπεισμαι ἐγὼ ἑκὼν εἶναι μηδένα ἀδικεῖν ἀνθρώπων, ἀλλὰ ὑμᾶς τοῦτο οὐ πείθω· ὀλίγον γὰρ χρόνον ἀλλήλοις διειλέγμεθα.

---

[1] Cf. *Meno*, 99 C, καὶ γὰρ οὗτοι (*i.e.* statesmen) λέγουσι μὲν ἀληθῆ καὶ πολλά, ἴσασι δὲ οὐδὲν ὧν λέγουσιν with *Apol.* 22 C, καὶ γὰρ οὗτοι (*i.e.* poets) λέγουσι μὲν πολλὰ καὶ καλά, ἴσασιν δὲ οὐδὲν ὧν λέγουσι, and the respective contexts. *Meno*, 98 D, seems a deliberate correction of the words φύσει τινὶ in *Apol.* 22 C.

The general structure of the work was of course prescribed to its author by the facts of the trial. Socrates had made three speeches, the first or main speech before the verdict, the second, in which an alternative to the death-penalty was proposed by the convicted defendant, according to Attic procedure, and the third which is in the nature of an informal address to the jury after sentence was passed. If any substantial addition were to be made, the natural place to put it was in the first speech. This Plato probably realised before he started to write; and I hope to show that, of the three sections into which the first speech naturally divides itself, the first is far more nearly a reproduction of what Socrates said than the second and third. But I do not imagine that Plato had, at the outset, any very definite idea of how he would incorporate fresh matter in the first speech, and what degree of play he would allow to his creative imagination. Examination of the work tends to suggest rather that that question settled itself as he proceeded. I believe that Plato went this way to work in many, if not in most, of the dialogues: for although they have nearly always a real unity, it is not usually the sort of unity which results from a systematic pre-conceived plan. In one case, indeed, that of the *Phaedrus*, he has been unsuccessful in attaining real unity by this method, or lack of method, with the result that the dialogue has two subjects, Love and Rhetoric, which fall almost completely apart. At the outset of the *Apology* he probably aimed at nothing more, or little more, than a reproduction of Socrates' arguments in his own words, expanding perhaps and emphasising, adding the grace of his own literary skill to the blunter style of the actual speech. But a point came when he became dissatisfied with this, namely when he reached the interrogation of Meletus; from that point onward to the end of the first speech invention prevailed over reproduction; it had to prevail, as we shall see; but Plato found himself freed from the shackles that bound his fancy, and at the necessary cost of obliterating Socrates' defence against the second part of the indictment, he was at once compelled and enabled to describe his master as he saw him, and to give to his readers for all time the splendid pages which close the first speech.

This is perhaps the most convenient place for me to mention the brief exordium of the *Apology* (17 A–18 A). I find no reason to doubt, and some to believe, that it is very much what Socrates said. Riddell, in his edition, points out that it contains many of the commonplaces employed in forensic speeches, *e.g.* the plea of unfamiliarity

with law-courts, lack of oratorical ability, etc.,
and concludes that 'the subtle rhetoric of this
defence would ill accord with the historical Socrates'. But the passage does not strike me as
being subtle rhetoric at all: the points are all
thoroughly natural, the tone is sincere. I cannot
discern the parodying intention which Burnet de-
tects, nor can I believe that Socrates would have
felt this a suitable occasion for parody. When he
says ἀτεχνῶς οὖν ξένως ἔχω τῆς ἐνθάδε λέξεως, he
is not being 'ironical', he merely means that he
has never had occasion to speak in a law-court
before, since he has never been a party to a case
(this is clearly the meaning of νῦν ἐγὼ πρῶτον
ἐπὶ δικαστήριον ἀναβέβηκα, as Burnet says): he
does not mean that he has never been present at
a trial, and knows nothing of the methods of
courts and forensic oratory.

It is of course possible that Socrates was
familiar with the commonplaces laid down in the
rhetorical text-books; if so, there was no reason
why he should not apply some of them to his own
case. But that he is deliberately doing this is by
no means certain. The fact is that all the points
made grow quite naturally out of one another;
the whole substance indeed is 'I am not an experienced pleader, like my accusers: I shall just
tell the truth in plain language'. There was no

need either to study text-books, or to ponder over the tricks of professional orators and speech-writers, for this to suggest itself to Socrates.

In the *Protagoras* and *Gorgias* Socrates is emphatic in disclaiming oratorical ability: he can converse, but he dislikes set speeches and is no good at them; and it is commonly agreed that this is a historical feature. Would it not then be exceedingly natural that he should make the same disclaimer now, when he finds himself compelled to make a set speech?

CHAPTER IV

THE MEANING OF THE INDICTMENT

Before proceeding to substantiate and amplify the general account of the *Apology* which I have given, it is necessary to examine the meaning and implications of the indictment; we must know what charges Socrates had to answer before we attempt to discuss the answer which Plato represents him as having given.

There is no question as to the wording of the indictment. It is quoted by Diogenes Laertius[1] on the authority of Favorinus, who says that he had consulted the Athenian archives in the Metroon: ἀδικεῖ Σωκράτης οὓς μὲν ἡ πόλις νομίζει θεοὺς οὐ νομίζων, ἕτερα δὲ καινὰ δαιμόνια εἰσηγούμενος. ἀδικεῖ δὲ καὶ τοὺς νέους διαφθείρων. Xenophon[2] agrees precisely with the single exception of εἰσφέρων for εἰσηγούμενος.[3]

I propose to consider separately the two parts of this indictment, namely the charge of irreligion and that of corrupting the young. The former

[1] II, 40.

[2] *Mem.* I, § 1.

[3] PA, 24 B does not claim to give the indictment exactly.

itself falls into two halves, which I shall refer to as the negative and the positive half.

As regards the negative half I have no hesitation in following Wilamowitz[1] on the actual meaning of the words, though I do not wholly agree with his view of their implication. The meaning is, as he says, that Socrates 'treats the Gods as non-existent'; he adds that this might imply either theoretical disbelief or neglect of ritual duties; but that since the former would not technically constitute ἀσέβεια (under which crime Socrates' offence must have fallen to come within the jurisdiction of the King Archon) the reference cannot have been to theoretical disbelief. Could Socrates then, Wilamowitz asks, have been charged with neglecting ritual duties? 'Hardly. Plato does not think it worth while to defend him against that. Xenophon points it out as notorious that Socrates performed all his proper sacrifices. Hence the non-recognition of the Gods consists rather in the introduction of the new Daimonia, by which he is said to replace them.' In other words the negative half of the charge of irreligion gets all its real meaning, in Wilamowitz's view, from the positive half.

[1] *Platon*, I, p. 158, 'Die Anklage macht dem S. zum Verbrechen, dass er die Götter als nicht vorhanden behandelt'.

In the first place I must defend Wilamowitz's assertion that θεοὺς νομίζειν can, in itself, denote theoretical disbelief; this is unfortunately necessary, since Burnet denies it[1]; he asserts that it means 'to acknowledge the gods by giving them the worship prescribed by νόμος, use and wont', adding the corollary, 'The charge is one of nonconformity in religious practice, not of unorthodoxy in religious belief'.[2]

I hope that I may be excused for being very brief on this point. In Aristophanes, *Clouds*, 819, Strepsiades remonstrates with his son for swearing by Zeus in the well-known line, τὸ Δία νομίζειν ὄντα τηλικουτονί; but he does not, I imagine, mean 'What a fool you are to give the worship prescribed by use and wont to Zeus at your age'.

[1] In his first note on 24 c 1. To be strict, Burnet does not explicitly deny this, but he certainly denies it by implication, for (a) he omits to consider the possibility of it, and (b) in his note on 26 c 2 he assumes, without argument, that νομίζειν εἶναι θεούς has a different meaning.

[2] Similarly Valgimigli in his analysis (p. 14) speaks of 'mancata venerazione agli dei della patria', though in his translation he has the non-committal 'non riconoscere gli dei'. Valgimigli appears to adopt Burnet's view both here and in regard to the meaning of δαιμόνια as beyond question.

But if it be granted that θεοὺς νομίζειν in the indictment *can*, as far as Greek usage goes, mean 'to believe in the gods', does it in fact mean this? There are three later passages in the *Apology* which throw light on this question, 26 C, 29 A and 35 D.

26 C: Socrates here has just turned, in his examination of Meletus, to the religious charge, having disposed of the 'corruption' charge. After referring to the terms of the indictment (κατὰ τὴν γραφὴν ἣν ἐγράψω θεοὺς διδάσκοντα μὴ νομίζειν οὓς ἡ πόλις νομίζει), he says he wants this explained: ἐγὼ γὰρ οὐ δύναμαι μαθεῖν πότερον λέγεις διδάσκειν με νομίζειν εἶναί τινας θεούς...οὐ μέντοι οὕσπερ γε ἡ πόλις ἀλλὰ ἑτέρους...ἢ παντάπασί με φῂς οὔτε αὐτὸν νομίζειν θεοὺς τούς τε ἄλλους ταῦτα διδάσκειν. 'By quietly interpolating εἶναι, Socrates takes advantage of the ambiguity of νομίζω, which means "think" when followed by the accusative and infinitive'[1] (Burnet). It seems odd that after four lines νομίζειν θεοὺς (without εἶναι) reappears. I submit that any unprejudiced reader of the passage from 26 B 2 to C 6 will

[1] It would seem that Xenophon though absent from the trial had this same bright thought of 'quietly interpolating εἶναι' at *Mem.* I, 1, § 5, πιστεύων δὲ θεοῖς πῶς οὐκ εἶναι θεοὺς ἐνόμιζεν; but *ibid.* § 2, ὡς οὐκ ἐνόμιζεν οὓς ἡ πόλις νομίζει θεούς.

admit that θεοὺς νομίζειν and θεοὺς νομίζειν εἶναι mean precisely the same here.

29 A: Socrates is saying that if he ran away from the post assigned him by God through fear of death or anything else, then certainly it would be just to bring him before a court, 'on the ground that I do not believe that the gods exist' (τότ' ἄν με δικαίως εἰσάγοι τις εἰς δικαστήριον, ὅτι οὐ νομίζω θεοὺς εἶναι). Would it not be pointless thus to formulate the charge in the hypothetical case, if in the actual case the charge did *not* denote disbelief in the *existence* of gods?

35 D: Socrates says that if by appeals for pity he forced the judges to vote against their true judgment when on oath, θεοὺς ἂν διδάσκοιμι μὴ ἡγεῖσθαι ὑμᾶς εἶναι, καὶ ἀτεχνῶς ἀπολογούμενος κατηγοροίην ἂν ἐμαυτοῦ ὡς θεοὺς οὐ νομίζω. Is it not plain that here μὴ ἡγεῖσθαι θεοὺς εἶναι and θεοὺς οὐ νομίζω (μὴ νομίζειν) are used synonymously, and that both refer to the terms and the meaning of the indictment?

If this is so, we must reject Wilamowitz's assertion that, although the phrase θεοὺς οὐ νομίζοντα might in itself refer to 'theoretical disbelief', yet it cannot in fact have this reference, since this would not constitute ἀσέβεια. The plain truth is that we do not know what the law of ἀσέβεια in 399 was. But we do not need to look beyond the last two quoted passages of the *Apology* itself to prove that disbelief in the existence of the gods came under that law. For whether we believe that Plato is repeating Socrates' own words in these two passages, or fathering them on Socrates, in either case it would be impossible to refer to the possibility of Socrates being prosecuted for disbelief in the existence of gods unless he could in fact have been prosecuted therefor. Nobody, I imagine, supposes that if this was an indictable offence, it came under some other law than the law of ἀσέβεια.

Of course it is not to be supposed that a man could be prosecuted for the mere holding of opinions to which he had not given expression in speech or writing: I only make this obvious remark in view of the fact that Burnet, referring in his first note on 24 c 1 to the case of Diagoras of Melos, seems to suggest that prosecution of a man for his opinions, as opposed to his utterance of them, is conceivable.

We may then take it as established that the negative half of the irreligion charge imputes to Socrates the expression of disbelief in the deities recognised by the State. Incidentally, we have rid ourselves of the necessity, which Wilamowitz finds, of supposing that the negative half has no real meaning in itself, but only finds one in conjunction with the positive half, *i.e.* that the non-recognition of the State gods consists entirely in the introduction of the καινὰ δαιμόνια.

We have now to consider the question, on what ground the prosecution alleged this disbelief. For an answer to this we shall look in vain to Xenophon. But PA, although it does not give a direct answer, yet indicates I think beyond all reasonable doubt what the answer must be. The ground of this charge was Socrates' supposed interest in the speculations of the Ionian φυσικοί. That this is so appears from a comparison of 18 C with 23 D–E. In the former passage Socrates says that those who hear the libels of his 'old accusers' to the effect that he is τά τε μετέωρα φροντιστὴς κτλ. are of opinion that those who inquire into such matters οὐδὲ θεοὺς νομίζειν. In the latter passage, he says that 'investigation of the things in the heavens and under the earth' and 'disbelief in gods' and 'making the worse cause the better' are imputations cast indiscriminately κατὰ πάντων τῶν φιλοσοφούντων, that they have been cast upon him by the people who resented being cross-examined by his young followers, and that on the strength of these imputations Meletus, Anytus and Lycon have brought him to trial.

It might, no doubt, be argued that by attributing

these charges to the 'old accusers' Socrates, or Plato, means that they were not in fact brought forward at the trial. But while recognising the force of this argument we must be guided by the probabilities of the case. I wish so far as possible to keep it for the present an open question whether this first section of the *Apology* (down to 24 c) is or is not substantially what Socrates said; but in either case I think we must believe that the prejudice which Socrates is exposing did really exist; people did believe that he was a nature-philosopher, a 'Sophist', and a disbeliever in the gods: I cannot see why either he, or Plato, should have invented the existence of this prejudice. And if that was so, why should the actual prosecutors have failed to exploit it? What I think most likely is that they exploited it rather by implication and innuendo than by definite statements. They were in the position of counsel who cannot afford to discard a point which he knows to be false, who realises that the prisoner (or opposing counsel) can refute it if it is made openly, and who therefore works mainly by the force of suggestion and implication. Anytus no doubt, and Meletus probably, knew well enough that Socrates was no μετεωροσοφιστής: but they probably did not foresee that their oblique references to μετεωροσοφία would be exposed by Socrates himself. They would say to themselves, as Schanz said,[1] that no accused person will strengthen the case against himself by introducing additional charges; and, if he did not do that, their 'suggestion' would bear its expected fruit.

It should be noted that Socrates does not suggest that the charge of introducing καινὰ δαιμόνια springs from the same source, from his supposed concern with natural science: it is only the negative half of the charge of irreligion that he traces to his old accusers.

We now pass to the positive half of the religious charge, that of introducing καινὰ δαιμόνια. Here again we must examine both the meaning and the implication of the words. As regards εἰσηγούμενος I am content to refer to A. S. Ferguson's paper in *C.Q.* VII (1913), which shows that the word does not mean to 'import from abroad', and therefore lends no support to the theory first advanced by Professor Taylor in *Varia Socratica*, and revived tentatively by Burnet in his second note on 24 c 1, that Socrates was accused for practising the religion of Pythagoreanism.[2] But does καινὰ δαιμόνια mean new or

[1] In the introduction to his edition of the *Apology*, p. 71, quoted in Burnet's introductory note.

[2] Mr Ferguson's paper exempts me from the need to discuss this theory.

strange *deities*, or new or strange *religious observances*? The former is the traditional view, and is I think generally[1] adopted still; the latter is held by Burnet and Professor Taylor. I do not think it is necessary to argue this point at great length: the well-known passage in *Euthyphro*, 3 B 2, is strongly in favour of the traditional view, and Xenophon *Apology*, § 24, seems to me decisive: it is not merely the case that, as Burnet admits, Xenophon understood δαιμόνια καινὰ to *imply* 'strange gods': he clearly understood it to *mean* that. Moreover, if my interpretation of θεοὺς νομίζειν is correct, it becomes obvious that Plato also, when writing the *Apology*, understood it to mean that; for the participle νομίζοντα in 24 C 1 governs δαιμόνια καινὰ as well as θεούς, and must be used in the same sense in relation to both its objects: and to translate 'believing in the existence of strange religious observances' is nonsense. As to Burnet's assertion that δαιμόνιον is never a substantive in Classical Greek, I am quite ready to believe that it became one *ad hoc*: the prosecutors wanted an unusual word which would suggest both that the gods that

[1] Wilamowitz accepts it, as is apparent from his remark, 'Also liegt die Nichtachtung der Götter vielmehr in der Einführung der neuen daimonia, die an ihre Stelle treten sollen' (*Platon*, I, p. 158).

Socrates believed in were no true gods, and that
τὸ δαιμόνιον which Socrates was always talking
about was the chief of them. The distinction between adjectives and substantives in Greek was
not so rigid that they could not use the plural
adjective in the sense required.

Having settled the meaning of the words, I
turn to their implication. What were the new or
strange 'deities' in which Socrates was accused
of believing? Here again I believe that all our
evidence points to the traditional view that the
Divine Sign was primarily alluded to.[1] That evidence must be so familiar to all readers of this
essay that I hardly need quote it in full: the
most important passages are *Euthyphro*, 3 B, and
Apology, 31 D. To the excellent remarks of Valgimigli, pp. 17–18, and Phillipson,[2] pp. 285–90,
I would only add one point. The only way of
getting round the statement of 31 C–D, where Socrates says that the cause of his abstention from
politics is what his hearers have often heard him
speak of, the fact, ὅτι μοι θεῖόν τι καὶ δαιμόνιον
γίγνεται, ὃ δὴ καὶ ἐν τῇ γραφῇ ἐπικωμῳδῶν Μέλητος ἐγράψατο is to understand the δή, as Burnet

[1] Even Valgimigli, though he follows Burnet un-
questioningly with regard to the *meaning* of νομίζοντα
and of καινὰ δαιμόνια, deserts him at this point (p. 17).

[2] Coleman Phillipson, *The Trial of Socrates* (1928).

does, to be ironical. Now, as Burnet himself points out, the turn of phrase is exactly like that of 19 B 1, ἡ ἐμὴ διαβολή...ἧ δὴ καὶ πιστεύων Μέλητός με ἐγράψατο τὴν γραφὴν ταύτην. But is *this* δή ironical? That it is not is proved by 23 E, where Socrates again brings the indictment of Meletus into connexion with the διαβολή in words which have no trace of irony, but are plainly intended to be taken in all seriousness: ἅτε οὖν οἶμαι φιλότιμοι ὄντες καὶ σφοδροὶ καὶ πολλοί...ἐμπεπλήκασιν ὑμῶν τὰ ὦτα καὶ πάλαι καὶ σφοδρῶς διαβάλλοντες. ἐκ τούτων ('on the strength of this') καὶ Μέλητός μοι ἐπέθετο κτλ.

In both places then it is clear that δή is not ironical, but means *profecto*. Burnet, indeed, holds (*Greek Philosophy*, Part I, p. 184) that the Sign *could* not have been the basis of this charge. 'The belief in possession (κατοκωχή) was much too firmly established, and cases of it were much too familiar, to allow of a charge of irreligion being based on anything of the kind.' But surely Xenophon must be a better judge of the *possibility* than any modern scholar; he may, or may not, be wrong about the fact; but he could not have suggested what he does unless it was a plausible interpretation of the charge.

Granting then that δαιμόνια καινά alludes primarily to the Divine Sign, why is the plural

used? Possibly it is mere vagueness or looseness of expression.[1] A more satisfactory explanation, however, suggests itself. Is it not *a
priori* likely that the prosecutors would employ
the supposed belief of Socrates in the deities of
the Ionian φυσικοί not merely in support of the
negative part of the religious charge, but in support of the positive part also? I should suppose
that their plan was, not to deal distinctly and
separately with the two parts but to run them
together. This suggestion finds some degree of
confirmation in Xenophon, *Mem.* I, 1, § 2, where
after mentioning the δαιμόνιον he adds ὅθεν δὴ
καὶ μάλιστά μοι δοκοῦσιν αὐτὸν αἰτιάσασθαι καινὰ
δαιμόνια εἰσφέρειν, 'this I think was the *principal*
ground for the charge of introducing strange
deities': there was another, subsidiary, ground
which Xenophon had heard mentioned. If this is
right, it was only natural for the plural to be
used in the indictment.

I now turn to the charge of corrupting the
young.

[1] Cf. Phillipson, p. 289, 'it was very easy to give
a slight twist to his expression and turn it into δαιμόνια,
divinities—indeed καινὰ δαιμόνια, new divinities—
notwithstanding the fact that he never used the word
as a substantive nor in the plural, meaning a divine
being or beings'.

It is well known that Xenophon devotes the second chapter of the first book of his *Memorabilia* to examining certain alleged methods of corrupting the young which had been brought up against Socrates by 'the accuser' (ὁ κατήγορος). It was first argued by Cobet, and is nowadays generally admitted, that the reference is not to Meletus or his associates in the prosecution, but to the Sophist Polycrates who, as has been mentioned, published his pamphlet against Socrates, which took the form of a speech by Anytus, sometime between 394 and 387. How far Xenophon believed that the allegations in question were also made at the trial it is impossible to say: though his careful omission to point out that 'the accuser' is a later writer leads one to suspect that he wished to give readers the impression that he is referring to the trial itself. The points made are four: (1) inculcation of disrespect for parents, relations and friends, (2) incitement to despise the established constitution and laws, and consequent encouragement of violence or revolutionary tendencies,[1] (3) mischievous interpretation of the poets, (4) responsibility for the mischief done to the State by his associates (ὁμιληταί), Critias and Alcibiades.

In his paper already referred to H. Gomperz

[1] *Mem.* 1, 2, § 9, καὶ ποιεῖν βιαίους.

has pointed out that Xenophon's method of dealing with these charges is to admit their foundation in fact in each case, while contesting the false and malicious twists given to the facts and the wrong inferences drawn from them. Xenophon, he concludes, would not have admitted these things as facts unless they were facts; incidentally it should be noticed that one of the points, namely inculcation of disrespect for parents, is already mentioned by Xenophon in *Apology*, § 20, before the composition of Polycrates' pamphlet, as having been brought up by Meletus at the trial. Now it would be rash to argue that all these points were used by Meletus and Anytus. In particular, reference to Socrates' association with Critias and Alcibiades could not, in view of the terms of the amnesty of 403 and of Anytus' undoubted loyalty towards it, have been openly referred to, though it may quite well have been hinted at. It is also quite possible that points other than those drawn by Xenophon from Polycrates were made, *e.g.* Socrates' challenging of traditional belief and authority in matters of conduct, his unsettling of young men's minds by insisting on their examination of moral concepts, his 'mischievous' doctrine that nobody does wrong voluntarily; good capital could have been made out of such matters. It would be of great interest to know whether Socrates was openly attacked for hostility to the democracy. So far as the amnesty was concerned there can have been nothing to preclude this, since Socrates is not likely to have given less offence in this respect since 403 B.C. than before that year. And if, as is generally supposed, the real motive behind the prosecution was political, if namely the leaders of the restored democracy felt nervous of Socrates as a political critic, there was nothing to prevent their showing their hand. Such evidence as we have, however, seems to give little or no support to this view of the motive of the prosecution. In the first place, the evidence of the *Apology* itself is against it. Socrates is made to say, repeatedly and emphatically, that his real danger of conviction springs, not from anything said by the actual present accusers, but from the long-standing prejudice against him as philosopher and sophist, as one who disbelieved in the gods and made the weaker cause the stronger. Now, if the real offence had been μισοδημία I cannot see why either Socrates should have said this, or Plato have represented him as saying it; on either hypothesis it seems pointlessly untrue. If anti-democratic sentiments and teaching were what Socrates was attacked for, it was surely what the judges were most likely to convict him for, even granting (though, as I have said, I see no reason to do so) that the prosecutors' actual speeches ignored or disguised the real point of attack. Again, when Plato has occasion to mention the trial of Socrates some forty-five years later, although the context is such that a reference to political motives would have been naturally expected, if they had been operative, he speaks of 'impiety' alone as the ground of accusation.[1]

[1] *Epistle*, VII, 325 B, κατὰ δέ τινα τύχην αὖ τὸν ἑταῖρον ἡμῶν Σωκράτη τοῦτον δυναστεύοντές τινες εἰσάγουσιν εἰς δικαστήριον, ἀνοσιωτάτην αἰτίαν ἐπιβαλόντες καὶ πάντων ἥκιστα Σωκράτει προσήκουσαν· ὡς ἀσεβῆ γὰρ οἱ μὲν εἰσήγαγον, οἱ δὲ κατεψηφίσαντο καὶ ἀπέκτειναν κτλ. This should surely outweigh the casual remark made by Aeschines (I, 173), ὑμεῖς, ὦ ἄνδρες Ἀθηναῖοι, Σωκράτην μὲν τὸν σοφιστὴν ἀπεκτείνατε, ὅτι Κριτίαν ἐφάνη πεπαιδευκώς, ἕνα τῶν τριάκοντα τῶν τὸν δῆμον καταλυσάντων. All this proves is that, in order to make a point against his opponent, the orator mentions an explanation of Socrates' execution which was current—though to what extent, we cannot say—in the middle of the 4th century. Everyone knows that the speeches of Athenian orators abound in falsifications of historical fact; and, apart from that, Aeschines may well have based his views on the pamphlet of Polycrates, or on Theodectes' *Apology of Socrates*, which must have appeared about this time. In any case it is illegitimate to treat such a remark as the assertion of an incontrovertible fact, as has frequently been done.

In the *Gorgias*,[1] when Socrates foresees that he may be brought to trial for corrupting the young, it is the unsettling, perplexing effect of his dialectic, with its 'bitter draughts' of salutary but unwelcome counsel, that he imagines as giving ground for the charge; the whole passage implies that Plato, at this date (*c.* 387 B.C.) believed that it was the ethical, not the political, side of Socrates' teaching that gave offence and led to the charge of διαφθορὰ τῶν νέων. Moreover this is fully in accord with the one and only passage in the *Apology* in which an argument used by Anytus is referred to. At 29 c Socrates says that Anytus had told the court that, now that the case has been brought to court, the death-penalty must be insisted upon, 'for if I were to escape, your sons would put into practice what Socrates teaches them, and would all be utterly corrupted'. The passage has all the appearance of a genuine quotation, and the language is certainly such as to suggest *moral* corruption, the effect of Socrates' teaching on the individual's

---

[1] 521 E–522 B, especially the opening words of the imaginary accuser: πολλὰ ὑμᾶς καὶ κακὰ ὅδε εἴργασται ἀνὴρ καὶ αὐτούς, καὶ τοὺς νεωτάτους ὑμῶν διαφθείρει τέμνων τε καὶ κάων, καὶ ἰσχναίνων καὶ πνίγων ἀπορεῖν ποιεῖ, πικρότατα πώματα διδοὺς κτλ. And later, ἐάν τέ τίς με ἢ νεωτέρους φῇ διαφθείρειν ἀπορεῖν ποιοῦντα κτλ.

conduct. What Anytus feared, and regarded as socially dangerous, was in fact the encouragement given by Socrates to young people to examine the principles of their behaviour and their moral judgments; to him and no doubt to many other honest patriots, this was the road to moral licence and social anarchy. To Anytus Socrates, like other sophists, seemed (to use his own words in the *Meno*[1]) 'the ruin and corruption of those who associate with him'. This was quite dangerous enough, and much more dangerous than the criticisms which Socrates was known to have uttered against certain Athenian institutions, such as the selection of officials by lot. It may be doubted whether Socrates' hostility to democracy was very pronounced, and we must not form our estimate of it from the Platonic Socrates of *Republic*, VIII.[2]

[1] 91 C, φανερὰ λώβη τε καὶ διαφθορὰ τῶν συγγιγνομένων.

[2] The hint given by Anytus at *Meno* 95 A, that Socrates will one day suffer for 'speaking ill of people' lends no support to the theory of political offence. Indeed it seems strange that Burnet should find such support (see his note on *Apology*, 18 B 3) in a dialogue in which Socrates expresses a surprisingly favourable judgment on Athenian politicians *as such*. In the immediately preceding context he has been pointing out that many prominent Athenian statesmen have

Once we discard the hypothesis of political motive, there seems no reason to suppose that one side of the indictment was stressed by the

failed, not as politicians, but as fathers, and it is as a father that Anytus feels himself implicitly reproached. It seems probable that one point made on the διαφθορά charge was that Socrates criticised the competence of parents to educate their children aright; hence in the *Gorgias* passage already quoted (522 B) the words ἐάν τέ τίς με ἢ νεωτέρους φῇ διαφθείρειν ἀπορεῖν ποιοῦντα are followed by ἢ τοὺς πρεσβυτέρους κακηγορεῖν λέγοντα πικροὺς λόγους. Of course 'abuse of the old' could not be made a formal ground of indictment, as the parallelism here if taken quite literally would suggest, but it could quite well be brought under that of 'corruption of the young'.

The πικροὶ λόγοι are the διατριβαί and λόγοι of *Apology*, 37 C–D: πολλὴ μεντᾶν με φιλοψυχία ἔχοι...εἰ οὕτως ἀλόγιστός εἰμι ὥστε μὴ δύνασθαι λογίζεσθαι ὅτι ὑμεῖς μὲν...οὐχ οἷοί τε ἐγένεσθε ἐνεγκεῖν τὰς ἐμὰς διατριβὰς καὶ τοὺς λόγους, ἀλλ᾽ ὑμῖν βαρύτεραι γεγόνασιν καὶ ἐπιφθονώτεραι, ὥστε ζητεῖτε αὐτῶν νυνὶ ἀπαλλαγῆναι.

I have not thought it necessary to refer to *Politicus*, 299 B–C, because it seems plain to me that what the Eleatic stranger there says has nothing to do with Socrates; if it had, we should have to suppose that Plato is *endorsing* the view of Socrates' prosecutors, for the stranger is laying down penal regulations (a point which might with advantage have been mentioned in Burnet's note on 24 B 9).

prosecution more than the other, or that Anytus
was the real mover in the proceedings and Meletus more or less his tool. The words attributed
to Anytus at 29 c incline me rather (though I
would not press this) to believe that Meletus was
not only nominal prosecutor but real originator
of the prosecution: for they suggest that Anytus
expressed some doubt as to the propriety or
wisdom of bringing the case into court.[1] It is
true that Plato, in the passage above quoted from
Epistle VII, speaks of the charge being brought
by δυναστεύοντές τινες, but that may well be a
natural looseness of expression signifying that
Anytus carried most weight, as of course he did.[2]
We may suppose that Meletus, no doubt the same
Meletus who spoke against Andocides on another
ἀσέβεια charge in this same year, and possibly
the speaker of Lysias' speech *Against Andocides*,
succeeded in working upon Anytus' apprehensions
of Socrates as a social danger. Between them they
formulated the indictment, in which the religious
charges were left mainly to Meletus, the social
mainly to Anytus: the part played by Lycon, the
other συνήγορος, is unknown. It is however quite

[1] ὃς ἔφη ἢ τὴν ἀρχὴν οὐ δεῖν ἐμὲ δεῦρο εἰσελθεῖν ἤ,
ἐπειδὴ εἰσῆλθον κτλ.

[2] Similarly I would understand τοὺς ἀμφὶ Ἄνυτον
(not Μέλητον) in *Apology*, 18 B.

possible that Meletus, as chief prosecutor, dealt to some extent with the social charge also: and he may well have represented Socrates' 'atheistic' teaching as part of the corruption of youth.

It has often been asked why Socrates was left alone so long, and only brought to trial at the age of 70. This we shall never know, and we must be content to accept Plato's words (*Ep.* VII, 325 B) that it was κατά τινα τύχην.

CHAPTER V

THE DEFENCE OF THE PLATONIC SOCRATES

The defence of the Platonic Socrates

(1) *On the irreligion charge*

I now turn to the question of the defence made by the Platonic Socrates to these charges. To what extent are the charges met in the main speech (the speech before the verdict), and how far can we believe that Plato has preserved Socrates' reply to them?

First, as to the negative half of the irreligion charge. If the interpretation of this has been right, the Socrates of the *Apology* has met it straightforwardly, naturally, and completely in the first section of the main speech (18 A–24 B). The manner of life that he has always pursued caused him long ago to be confounded in the minds of his fellow-citizens, whether through malice or through genuine misconception, with the natural philosophers and the 'Sophists'[1]: the

---

[1] Here, as often in the Socratic literature, there is no clear line drawn between the φυσικοί and the σοφισταί. Popular opinion certainly lumped them all together as σοφοί ('high-brows').

comic poets, particularly Aristophanes, gave currency to this misconception. Socrates denies it in simple and forceful language, himself distinguishing (as his traducers had neglected to distinguish) between φυσικοί and σοφισταί and discriminating his own quest of σοφία from that of both these classes. In so far as these pages bring out what Socrates was *not*, I can see no reason to doubt that Plato is faithfully preserving the substance of Socrates' defence. Not only is the whole account of the διαβολή and the 'old accusers' natural and convincing, but it is unlikely that Plato should have invented a line of defence which goes far to shift the odium of Socrates' execution from the actual accusers and judges themselves on to the nameless representatives of a bygone generation. There is, I believe, nowhere else either in Plato's writings or elsewhere any suggestion that Socrates had long been the victim of popular misrepresentation. When Plato in his old age is recounting[1] the circumstances which led him to abandon his early ambitions for a political career, he refers to the prosecution of Socrates as the crime of δυναστεύοντές τινες without any hint that it was the inevitable outcome of decades of popular ill-will. The pages in question, however, give at least

[1] *Ep.* VII, 325 B–C.

equal prominence to the *positive* account of what Socrates *was*, in what sense he was σοφός or φιλό-σοφος, and in this I believe that some measure of Platonic invention is to be detected.[1]

Next as to the positive half of the irreligion charge. It has often been remarked, and it is indeed remarkable, that the *Apology* contains no reply, or at least no formal and direct reply, to the charge of introducing καινὰ δαιμόνια. The nearest approach to a reply is given in the course of the interrogation of Meletus at 27 B–D. But, quite apart from the fact that this interrogation seems to be, as I shall argue later, almost wholly Platonic invention, this passage does not really constitute an answer to the *positive* charge. It is true that Socrates here makes use of the phrase δαιμόνια νομίζειν, but the argument ignores the καινά of the indictment, and is in fact a dialectical rebuttal of the *negative* charge, for it aims at proving, not that Socrates did not introduce strange gods, but that he believed in gods.

It may no doubt be argued that the whole account of Socrates' divine mission—the constantly recurring theme of the main speech (apart from the interrogation section)—is in effect a reply, and the best reply that could have been given: the lifelong servant of Apollo is hardly a be-

[1] See pp. 88 ff. *infra.*

liever in strange gods. In a sense this is true: nevertheless it does seem strange that, whereas the negative half of the irreligion charge has been fully met by exposing it as merely an echo or revival of the old διαβολή, the positive half should be met only in this indirect fashion. In particular it seems strange that the δαιμόνιον itself should be mentioned once only,[1] quite incidentally, at 31 D.

It is suggested by Wilamowitz that Socrates could not satisfactorily answer the charge, and that he endeavoured to cover up the 'weak point' by the dialectical argument with Meletus, 27 B–D, which is not seriously meant, but is only calculated to raise a laugh at Meletus' expense. With this I disagree, because it was perfectly possible for Socrates to defend himself on the Xenophontic line, by arguing that his Sign was only a special and unobjectionable form of μαντική: indeed the agreement of the Xenophontic defence with PA, 40 A (ἡ εἰωθυῖά μοι μαντικὴ ἡ τοῦ δαιμονίου), makes it probable that he did so regard it.

Nor am I satisfied with the suggestion that Socrates disdained to reply to the actual charges because they were patently false and malicious: for, as I have said, he does answer the negative

[1] The reference to it in the third speech (40 A) is of course irrelevant to the present question.

charge fully and directly. It is a mistake to think that the 'serious defence' begins only at 28 A: there has been a serious defence against the negative charge in 18 A–24 C.

My belief is that the absence of defence against the positive charge is to be found in the situation existing when the *Apology* was written. I suggest that by that time the absurdity of finding 'impiety' in Socrates' δαιμόνιον had become patent; whether Xenophon had by then written and published the first chapter of his *Memorabilia* we cannot be certain, though I do not think it is likely. But he had certainly written his *Apology*, in which the δαιμόνιον is defended (§§ 12–13) substantially as in the *Memorabilia*. We may well hesitate to attribute to Xenophon's work the realisation by the general public of the truth on this matter; I am more disposed to think that Socrates himself convinced his judges on this point at the trial. However that may be, the silence of Plato's *Apology* loses its difficulty if we assume that the truth about the δαιμόνιον was known when he wrote it, and that therefore he did not hold it necessary to reproduce this part of Socrates' defence, which may well moreover have been quite brief. This explanation becomes, I think, more acceptable if I am right in supposing that the 'Ionian gods' had been brought in to

support the positive charge as well as the negative: for Plato would feel that in reproducing
Socrates' rebuttal of the negative charge he had
ipso facto dealt with the only part of the positive
charge which still merited rebuttal.

'Socrates the Meteorosophist' still remained
an object of suspicion: his own speech in court
had not availed to destroy that figure in the
minds of many of the Athenians who discussed
the celebrated trial: we may probably hear an
echo of these persistent discussions in the sections
(*Mem.* I, 1, §§ 11–16) in which Xenophon seems
to exaggerate,[1] for apologetic purposes, the dislike which Socrates felt for the φυσικοί.

By the time that Polycrates came to write his
attack on Socrates, which we can probably date
not much earlier than 387, it would appear that
the whole attempt to justify the charge of irreligion had collapsed: for Polycrates, so far as we
know,[2] confined himself to the charge of corrupting the young.

[1] Cf. especially § 11, τοὺς φροντίζοντας τὰ τοιαῦτα
μωραίνοντας ἀπεδείκνυε; § 13, τοῖς μαινομένοις ὁμοίως
διακεῖσθαι πρὸς ἀλλήλους.

[2] This is indeed an almost certain inference from
Libanius.

(2) *On the corruption charge*

It cannot be said that any direct and formal reply is made to this charge. For the most part it is treated, as was the charge of introducing strange deities, indirectly: that is to say Socrates describes the true nature of his influence on his fellow-citizens, and from his description, particularly where he speaks of his life-work as an appeal to men to 'care for the soul' (30 B), the incredibility of the charge clearly emerges: εἰ μὲν οὖν ταῦτα λέγων διαφθείρω τοὺς νέους, ταῦτα ἂν εἴη βλαβερά. It is to be noted that this passage belongs to the *third* section of the main speech, a section which, as we shall see later, is not presented by Plato as part of Socrates' formal ἀπολογία, this being concluded at 28 A. In addition to the passage just mentioned, this third section contains, at 33 D, a challenge to anyone in court, or to their relatives, to come forward and give evidence substantiating the charge of corruption, and at 33 B Socrates makes an indirect allusion to the charge by disclaiming responsibility for the moral failings of those who are wrongly called his 'disciples'. Plainly none of these passages contains any rebuttal of the specific points which must have been made in the speeches for the prosecution. And the same is true of the one and only

passage in the *first* section of the main speech
(that section which precedes the examination of
Meletus), in which the corruption charge is
alluded to, viz. at 23 c–d: there Socrates speaks
of it, not with direct reference to the formal indictment, but as a random charge levelled against
him in popular talk by persons smarting under
the ἐξέτασις of his own followers who employed
his own methods: ἐντεῦθεν οὖν οἱ ὑπ᾽ αὐτῶν ἐξετα-
ζόμενοι ἐμοὶ ὀργίζονται, οὐχ αὑτοῖς, καὶ λέγουσιν
ὡς Σωκράτης τίς ἐστι μιαρώτατος καὶ διαφθείρει
τοὺς νέους. The only place in the *Apology* where
Socrates even purports to face the corruption
charge directly, not by indirect rebuttal or casual
allusion, is in the interrogation of Meletus. This
interrogation-section I shall have to deal with
separately, and it will appear that not even here
is there any real reply made to a definite charge:
the treatment is general, verbal, dialectical.

Now I regard it as highly improbable that
Socrates did in fact ignore the definite points
made by the prosecution in substantiation of
their charge. More particularly it seems incredible that he can have claimed, as Plato represents
him claiming, at 28 a, *before the third section*,
which alone contains that indirect substitute for
a refutation which I have noticed above, that
he has already dealt adequately with the *whole*

indictment, that is to say with the corruption charge as well as the charge of irreligion.

Why then has Plato omitted this part of Socrates' defence? This question does not seem to admit of more than a tentative answer, and the suggestion which I would make will be more conveniently postponed until after we have considered the second section of the main speech, namely that containing the interrogation of Meletus. But before we come to that it is necessary to give some further consideration to the first section, in order to determine how far the positive description of Socrates' mission, which is there bound up with the refutation of the irreligion charge, betrays Platonic invention.

The Delphic Oracle

It will be generally agreed that the central theme of Socrates' first speech, and indeed of the whole *Apology*, is his consciousness of a divine mission to his fellow-men. It would be superfluous to quote the numerous passages in which he describes himself as obeying a divine command, as ordering his whole life in such obedience, as determined not to quit his post, where God has stationed him. God had spoken to him through the Delphic oracle, which declared in

answer to the question of Chaerephon that no
man was wiser than Socrates. Puzzled by this
oracle, he at first thinks that he will refute it,
will prove it to be false (21 B, ἦλθον ἐπί τινα τῶν
δοκούντων σοφῶν εἶναι, ὡς ἐνταῦθα εἴπερ που
ἐλέγξων τὸ μαντεῖον καὶ ἀποφανῶν τῷ χρησμῷ ὅτι
'Οὑτοσὶ ἐμοῦ σοφώτερός ἐστι, σὺ δ' ἐμὲ ἔφησθα').
After successively interrogating statesmen, poets
and artisans, he discovered what the oracle must
have meant: that *he* is the wisest of men whoever
(like Socrates) knows that he has no wisdom.

Already, in the course of this account, Socrates
has described himself as searching, or inquiring,
'in accordance with the god's bidding' (22 A,
ζητοῦντι κατὰ τὸν θεόν); and at the close of the
account he says 'So that is why I still, even to-day,
go about searching and examining, in accordance
with the god's bidding, any citizen or stranger
whom I fancy to be wise' (23 B, ταῦτ' οὖν ἐγὼ μὲν
ἔτι καὶ νῦν περιιὼν ζητῶ καὶ ἐρευνῶ κατὰ τὸν θεὸν
καὶ τῶν ἀστῶν καὶ ξένων ἄν τινα οἴωμαι σοφὸν
εἶναι). And he continues, 'And when I find he is
not wise, by way of helping the god I demonstrate
to him that he is not' (καὶ ἐπειδάν μοι μὴ δοκῇ,
τῷ θεῷ βοηθῶν ἐνδείκνυμαι ὅτι οὐκ ἔστι σοφός).

Now it is by no means clear why Socrates
should speak of his examination of the reputed
wise men as obedience to the god. For in fact

his procedure sprang, as he himself asserts, from incredulity towards the oracle and a desire to prove it mistaken. It may perhaps be urged that Socrates felt that, although he was trying to prove it mistaken, he was in fact helping to prove it right, and that in this sense he was serving or 'helping' the god; it may be urged that what he says about his initial incredulity is typical Socratic irony. But even so we are no further towards understanding why Socrates should use the phrase κατὰ τὸν θεόν in connexion with his 'examination': it is one thing to 'help' the god in the sense of substantiating his oracle: it is another thing to execute the god's command. I can agree with Burnet when, in his note on βοηθῶν at 23 B, he says, 'Now that Socrates has discovered the true meaning of the oracle, he no longer seeks to refute it, but becomes the champion of the god', but I am as far as ever from understanding the words of the next sentence, καὶ ὑπὸ ταύτης τῆς ἀσχολίας...ἐν πενίᾳ μυρίᾳ εἰμὶ διὰ τὴν τοῦ θεοῦ λατρείαν.

And there is this further difficulty: even granting that Socrates might, illogically but perhaps intelligibly, have regarded his examination of the wise as obedience to a command, implied in or deduced from the oracle, to prove that oracle's truth, how can his lifelong continuance of his activity on the same lines, after he had substantiated it, be still explained as obedience? It may be replied that though he had substantiated it to his own satisfaction, it was still incumbent on him to substantiate it before others; but who will believe that Socrates really conceived his life's work to have consisted in substantiating an oracle before men who had most of them never heard of it? What a pitiable and absurd thing the sense of a divine mission would then become! And why do we find no trace in the Platonic dialogues of such an interpretation by Socrates of his service?

What solution then can be offered for these difficulties? To anticipate the conclusion of the argument which I shall put forward, I believe that Plato has caused them himself, not indeed by inventing the oracle (which Xenophon also reports, in a different form), not by inventing Socrates' proving and interpretation of the oracle: in all this I can find no ground for suspicion; Socrates may well have said all this, except for the phrases which make his 'Menschenprüfung' to be obedience to the oracle, or service of the god—but by *attempting to find in the oracle* the source of Socrates' consciousness that his life's work—of exposing men's vain conceit of wisdom (his 'elenchtic' activity) on the one hand, and of urging them to care for their souls or their moral welfare (his 'protreptic' activity) on the other hand—was prescribed and inspired by a divine Master.

What arguments can be adduced pointing to this conclusion?

(1) At 33 c, after saying that people like to follow him about because they enjoy hearing him examine those who think they are wise, he proceeds: ἐμοὶ δὲ τοῦτο, ὡς ἐγώ φημι, προστέτακται ὑπὸ τοῦ θεοῦ πράττειν καὶ ἐκ μαντείων καὶ ἐξ ἐνυπνίων καὶ παντὶ τρόπῳ ᾧπέρ τίς ποτε καὶ ἄλλη (? ἄλλῳ) θεία μοῖρα ἀνθρώπῳ καὶ ὁτιοῦν προσέταξε πράττειν. This seems to show that Plato has, at this point of the *Apology*, abandoned, or forgotten, the idea that the original oracle is the *sole* inspiration of Socrates' continued activity. No doubt it is quite legitimate to argue that Socrates might have rested his belief in a divine mission on these further signs as being *confirmatory* of the original command imposed by the first and all-important oracle. But then would it not have been natural, and indeed certain, that he would have referred to these later confirmatory signs when describing, earlier in the speech, the imperative aspect of the original oracle? The way to account for this is, I think, to believe that the passage in 33 c just quoted represents closely what Socrates did say: its inconsistency with the story of 21 B–

23 c disappears if we deduct from that story the element of the imperative in the oracle.

(2) The second reason for my conclusion is that it gets rid also of what many commentators, *e.g.* H. Gomperz and H. Maier, and in a lesser degree Wilamowitz, have felt as a difficulty, namely the unexpectedly great importance attached by Socrates to the utterance of the Pythian priestess. Opinions may no doubt differ on this point: some find no difficulty in believing that the religion of Socrates was of a completely orthodox type which would naturally lead him to accept any utterance of Delphi without a shadow of doubt: such is the view, *e.g.*, of E. Horneffer,[1] who devotes many eloquent and persuasive pages to its support. The more moderate view taken by Wilamowitz is that, although Plato has exaggerated the importance of the oracle for Socrates, yet Socrates might well have taken it as a welcome corroboration of a 'call' already felt through a more inward kind of religious experience. My own belief is that the suspicions of Gomperz, Maier and Wilamowitz on this score are well-founded: and that although Horneffer is well justified in protesting against older conceptions of an over-rationalist Socrates, yet he has gone too far in the other direction.

[1] In *Der junge Platon*.

Thus I should welcome any interpretation of the *Apology* which enabled us to disembarrass Socrates of an explanation of his life and his vocation in terms which seem inappropriate to a man who, while accepting the forms of traditional Greek religion, was yet not shackled by them. But we have really no need to rest the case on an admittedly debatable view of the nature of Socrates' religious belief, or the degree of his general orthodoxy: we can rest it on his particular procedure in this instance. His procedure in testing the oracle is incompatible with a serious acceptance of its authority: and the interpretation of its meaning at which he arrives is a *rationalistic* interpretation, a saving of Apollo's face by ingeniously imputing to him what he did not say. In short, Socrates' own treatment of the oracle—which, as I have said, there seems no reason to doubt is correctly reported by Plato—is itself evidence that he did not receive it in such a spirit as could make it possible for him to regard it as the voice of God, determining and ordering all his future activity. His interpretation of the oracle is a typical example of his accustomed irony: but his obedience to the voice of God, heard in the stillness of his own soul, without the intervention of a human medium, contained no element of irony: that was his profound conviction, reached by a religious experience that did not exclude, but embraced and confirmed, his rational judgment of the moral weakness of men.

I am not of course attempting to argue that Socrates attached no value to oracles, omens and visions. To maintain that would be flatly to contradict the evidence both of Xenophon and of Plato. As to Xenophon it is probably true, and I suppose generally believed, that he has projected into his Socrates something of his own naive orthodoxy, his 'engorthodoxe Frömmigkeit', as Horneffer styles it. But a Socrates wholly sceptical in regard to the traditional μαντική would never have found in Xenophon an admiring disciple and biographer.[1] As to Plato, we cannot believe that he has falsified the picture of Socrates to the extent implied. No: Socrates believed in divination as an integral part of that religious representation in which he had grown

[1] If the oracle given to Chaerephon really meant all that Plato tells us that it meant to Socrates, surely Xenophon would have heard Socrates speak of its supreme importance in his life, and would have been only too eager to record its importance. But the Xenophontic *Apology* treats the oracle in a wholly different fashion, and the *Memorabilia* is silent about it altogether.

up, and to which he clung because of the elements of value which he recognised in it. The very fact that he, like Euripides, was anxious to purge mythology of its unedifying elements, is enough to show that it never occurred to him to disbelieve in the existence of the gods of Olympus[1]: and unless he was a rank hypocrite he could not have been, as Xenophon tells us he was, punctilious in his religious duties if he had disbelieved. His sincere humility, which was one side of his εἰρωνεία, was incompatible with the attitude of the dogmatic free-thinker who hates free-thought and proclaims every religious belief that will not stand the test of his own individual reasoning to be a sham. He was, I think, content and wisely content not to attempt an explicit reconciliation of reason with faith; not out of indifference, nor in a spirit of complacent, condescending toleration of traditional belief, but rather because he possessed that rare wisdom which knows that, while no bounds may properly be set to the activity of human reason—that the ἀνεξέταστος βίος is οὐ βιωτὸς ἀνθρώπῳ—yet ἡ ἀνθρωπίνη σοφία ὀλίγου τινὸς ἀξία ἐστὶ καὶ οὐδενός.

If this interpretation is accepted, then we can-

[1] On this point see the thoroughly sound and sensible remarks of E. B. Osborn, *Socrates and his Friends*, pp. 145–51.

not admit the account of the *Apology* in so far as it attaches paramount importance to the oracle given to Chaerephon. How then are we to explain this feature of the defence?

Ivo Bruns, whose chapter on the *Apology*[1] is, it may be remarked, highly praised by Wilamowitz, holds that when Socrates (*i.e.* the Socrates created by Plato) begins to give an account of his life to a court which he knows to be for the most part hostile, and incapable of understanding him, he is unable at first to speak with full openness, and takes refuge in a romance or fairy-story; 'Er sagt die Wahrheit, aber er erzählt sie wie ein Märchen'. Later, however, he overcomes this embarrassment, and speaks out without the veil of fantasy. This embarrassed Socrates seems to me to exist only in Bruns' imagination: the first page of the *Apology* is enough to explode him: and indeed he prefaces the supposed 'Märchen' by saying ἴσως μὲν δόξω τισὶν ὑμῶν παίζειν· εὖ μέντοι ἴστε, πᾶσαν ὑμῖν τὴν ἀλήθειαν ἐρῶ (20 D), as if in anticipation of a Bruns.

A truer line of interpretation is represented by Wilamowitz. The gist of his view, contained in the chapter significantly entitled *Wahrheit und Dichtung*, is that Socrates found in the oracle a

[1] *Das literarische Porträt der Griechen*, Book III, chap. 1.

welcome confirmation from without of the inner conviction on which he had long been acting.[1] And, he adds, doubtless the oracle was no small solace for the discomforts which his vocation imposed upon him.

With this, so far as it goes, I am completely in agreement. But Wilamowitz has not raised the question which still remains, viz. why did Plato make so much more of the oracle than Socrates had made? The only attempts to answer this are, so far as I know, those of E. Wolff and H. Gomperz. Wolff suggests[2] that Plato wanted to represent the 'calling' of Socrates as analogous to Socrates' own 'calling' of others: just as he constantly set to his interlocutors the 'riddle' τί τὸ καλόν, τί τὸ ὅσιον, etc., so Apollo set to him the riddle (cf. τί ποτε αἰνίττεται, 21 b) 'What is wisdom?'; just as Socrates brings men to ἀπορία so he himself feels ἀπορία at the oracle (ἠπόρουν τί ποτε λέγει, ibid.).

This is ingenious, but not, I think, convincing. The explanation seems to break down on a vital point: the passages of the *Apology* in which Plato

[1] *Platon*, ii, p. 54, 'Dass er nun den inneren Beruf zu seiner Menschenprüfung auch äusserlich durch die anerkannte höchste Instanz der Wahrheitserkundung bestätigt erhalten hatte, war doch nichts Geringes'.

[2] *Neue Philolog. Untersuch.* vi (1929), pp. 72 ff.

describes Socrates' ἐξέτασις of his fellow-men
none of them picture him as seeking for defini-
tions of ethical terms; in other words, none of
them make him propound αἰνίγματα of the kind
which Wolff refers to. Wolff is, of course, thinking of the passage in Xenophon, *Mem.* I, 1, § 16,
αὐτὸς δὲ (in contrast with the φυσικοί) περὶ τῶν
ἀνθρωπείων ἀεὶ διελέγετο σκοπῶν τί εὐσεβές, τί
ἀσεβές, τί καλόν, τί αἰσχρόν, κτλ. Although it is
perfectly possible to reconcile this Xenophontic
account with the picture of Socrates' activity
given in the *Apology*—and the Xenophontic
account is of course confirmed by Plato in many
dialogues—yet Plato would surely have made
the Socrates of the *Apology* describe his ἐξέτασις
in the Xenophontic way if he had really intended
his readers to see a parallel between that activity
and Socrates' own 'calling' by the oracle.

Secondly, there is the explanation given by
H. Gomperz. As the result of a careful comparison of the Xenophontic and Platonic accounts
of Socrates' Divine Sign, Gomperz comes to the
conclusion that Plato has deliberately minimised
the significance of the Sign for apologetic purposes. Socrates, he holds, interpreted the Sign
as a direct communication from the supreme
deity: this supreme deity he called τὸ δαιμόνιον,
while recognising the individual gods of the

4340**9**

Olympic theology only as various names given to Him. It was on the consciousness that he was in constant communion, through the Sign, with this one true god that Socrates rested his belief in a divine mission. Plato, however, in view of the fact that the Sign was the object of attack by the prosecution, reduces it to something quite unimportant in the defence which he attributes to Socrates, robbing it of its tremendous religious significance, and substituting for it the oracle given to Chaerephon.

This theory is difficult to accept. For if the Sign was of the paramount importance suggested, then it is incredible that Socrates should not have explained that it was: for to have suppressed that all-important fact would have been impossible if, as both Plato and Xenophon assert and everyone believes, Socrates showed complete fearlessness at the trial, and was anxious to tell the truth about himself and his life-work. The supposed suppression would in fact be a gross *suggestio falsi*: for, whatever the religious charge meant, it meant something about Socrates' religion: and whatever answer he made to it, that answer must have made reference to the most important feature of Socrates' religious experience. But if Socrates did at the trial admit the paramount importance of the Sign, then it would have been purposeless, nay it would have been the height of folly, for Plato to suppress the admission. For everyone would have said, 'It is no use your making out that Socrates did not refer his whole activity to a religious experience which the court judged to be ἀσέβεια: for we heard him do it. You cannot hope to influence opinion in favour of Socrates by suppressing the most vitally important admission which he made in open court'.

The explanation which I would offer as a solution of the difficulty about the oracle is much simpler than those of Wolff and Gomperz. As I have said, the sole source of the difficulty is the *attachment of an imperative* to the interpretation of the oracle which Plato makes Socrates give. The attachment of that imperative I believe to be Plato's own doing: and his motive, I think, was a perfectly simple and a perfectly honest motive: he wanted to explain to himself and others why Socrates had believed himself to be sent by God to serve his people. Socrates had not given any explanation at the trial, and probably not at any time: why not? Because there was no explanation to give: he just believed it to be so. Plato thought, wrongly but not unnaturally, that there must have been an explanation, and that it was a pity that Socrates had not given it, because it would have impressed his judges favourably: when he came to write his *Apology*, in which, as I have argued, his purpose was to influence contemporary opinion in favour of Socrates, he thought that it would subserve that purpose if he showed that Socrates, accused of impiety, might have defended his life-work as obedience, not merely to God, but to God speaking through the mouth of the Pythian priestess.

It was very natural for Plato to think that this was in truth the missing explanation: for he knew that it was the oracle that had been the occasion of Socrates' embarking upon his 'elenchtic' task. That part of the story Plato did not invent: there is, as I have said, no reason to doubt that Socrates interpreted the pronouncement as to his 'wisdom' in the sense the *Apology* gives. Without reposing any implicit faith in it he said, 'If it is really true that nobody is wiser than I, it must be because I know my own ignorance': and so his conversations with all sorts of men thenceforward took the 'elenchtic' turn—he began to preface his moral talks with an ἐξέτασις or ἔλεγχός designed to convince his hearers of their ignorance of the fundamental things of life. But the 'calling' of Socrates, which had no external form, had come earlier; how early we do not know: but at all events there had been time enough to win the admiration of Chaerephon, who was doubtless only one amongst many disciples who would have put the same leading question at Delphi. Socrates had already[1] come to be recognised as 'wise', because he had already long been exhorting 'both citizens and strangers, and especially citizens' (30 A) μήτε σωμάτων ἐπιμελεῖσθαι μήτε χρημάτων πρότερον μηδὲ οὕτω σφόδρα ὡς τῆς ψυχῆς ὅπως ὡς ἀρίστη ἔσται.

Finally, before I leave this topic of the Delphic oracle, I must forestall an objection. It may be said that what I have been arguing is based on purely subjective criticism: that I have found, or rather others have found and I have repeated, a difficulty in Socrates' account of the oracle simply from a preconceived idea of what Socrates would and would not be likely to have said. To this I reply that before mentioning this particular difficulty, I had raised others (pp. 89 ff.) which are certainly not the creations of subjective criticism: and although I do believe that my proposed solution overcomes the last-mentioned difficulty, yet it does not stand or fall according as that difficulty is real or imaginary. In other words, even those who are perfectly satisfied with Socrates referring his whole activity to the

[1] See *infra*, pp. 154 ff.

voice of Delphi have still to explain the 'imperative element' in the oracle, and the passage quoted on p. 92 from 33 c.

The interrogation of Meletus.

The only part of the *Apology* in which Socrates *formally* deals with the indictment is at 24 c–27 e, the passage in which Meletus is subjected to interrogation. I have in the foregoing pages assumed that no real answer to the charge of irreligion is to be found here; but I must now examine this passage and determine its real purport.

The first point that must strike any reader here is that, though Socrates declares at 28 a that he has in the preceding three or four pages, *i.e.* in the interrogation section, adequately replied to the actual charges brought against him,[1] he does not in fact refute any definite allegations at all. His method is (*a*) to show that Meletus has not the least idea what he means by 'corrupting the young', and (*b*) to entrap him into contradicting himself about the meaning of the charge of irreligion. The whole passage is written as if nothing whatever had been said by the prosecutors by way of explaining or substan-

---

[1] ὡς μὲν ἐγὼ οὐκ ἀδικῶ κατὰ τὴν Μελήτου γραφήν, οὐ πολλῆς μοι δοκεῖ εἶναι ἀπολογίας, ἀλλὰ ἱκανὰ καὶ ταῦτα.

tiating the indictment; it is written exactly in the style of an imaginary dialogue intended to illustrate Socrates' dialectical skill. When Socrates asks Meletus at 26 B to tell the court what he means by 'corrupting the young', and without waiting for an answer suggests that it is plain *from the indictment* (κατὰ τὴν γραφὴν ἣν ἐγράψω) what he does mean, Meletus at once assents emphatically. And yet the suggestion is surely one which Meletus would not have assented to without some qualification; for it is plain that the indictment would not have had its actual form, in which the charge of corruption is carefully put forward as a *separate* charge from that of irreligion, if, as Socrates suggests, the corruption consisted in his teaching irreligious doctrines alone. It may be urged that Meletus might well lose his head when confronted by the terrifying ordeal of standing up to Socrates' questions; but even allowing that he might make the initial mistake of assenting to this suggestion, would he not at some later point have recovered himself and made some reference to the substantiation of the corruption charge that must have been given either in his own speech or that of Anytus? The fact is that Plato allows Socrates to conduct this dialogue to suit his own end; he makes Meletus always give just the answer that

Socrates wants, and no interruptions, no quali-
fications, no retractations of any unwary admis-
sions, are allowed. Does anyone suppose that
the rules of Athenian law-courts precluded such
corrections? Possibly in an English court, where
a witness is compelled to give direct answers to
counsel's questions, and an experienced judge is
alert to see that he does so and does nothing
else, Socrates might have carried off his succes-
sion of dialectical triumphs: and indeed I imagine
it is just because we unconsciously substitute
the practices of a modern for those of an ancient
law-court that this scene has been accepted as
real. Even so we should have to regard Meletus
as a pretty considerable fool. For who but a
fool would have fallen into the trap of calling
Socrates a believer in *no* gods (26 c, 26 e)? Even
if we granted what I have shown to be impossible,
that the word δαιμόνια in the indictment did not
actually *mean* 'divine beings', we cannot doubt
that the allegation of introducing strange καινὰ
δαιμόνια at least *implied* the recognition of
strange gods. Why then, when asked the plain
question whether what the prosecution allege is
belief in no gods whatever, does Meletus at once
assent, absolutely and without qualification?
What one would expect him to have said would
be either, 'You believe in what you call a god or

gods, but they are no true gods', or else 'I have explained that to the court in my speech'. If Socrates had been trying his dialectic on some chance-comer, who had given no attention to the point, no doubt we might think it reasonable for him to give the answer which Plato's Socrates wants, owing to a vague feeling that believing in false gods is the same thing as believing in none: but Meletus and Anytus together have drawn up a carefully worded charge which explicitly and deliberately avoids the identification of *false* belief with *no* belief. Again, if Meletus had any aptitude for his job he would not have allowed (25 A) that Socrates *alone* corrupted the young; he would have said that all those who had come under Socrates' pernicious influence spread the contagion; even supposing him to have fallen into this trap at 25 A, he might surely have interrupted to correct himself when subjected to the direct attack of 25 C: and no president of an Athenian court would have hindered him.

Why then did Plato write these pages? I think there were two reasons: first, he felt that no picture of Socrates could be adequate which did not contain an example of his dialectical ability; and if, as is quite likely and as Xenophon's *Apology* represents, there was in fact an interrogation in which Socrates scored some points against Meletus, he might well have been tempted (and contemporary standards would justify him) to exaggerate and enlarge the scope of his triumph. Secondly, there is reason to believe that Plato disliked and despised Meletus, and saw an opportunity of discrediting him at least with readers who had not been present at the trial. Every time Meletus is referred to there is some word of disparagement: at *Euthyphro*, 2 B, he is an 'unknown individual, with lanky hair, wispy beard, and hooked nose'[1]: while the following sentences (2 B–3 A) contain an elaborate sarcasm on his disinterested public spirit. At *Gorgias*, 521 c, he is 'an utterly bad and worthless person' (εἰσαχθεὶς εἰς δικαστήριον ὑπὸ πάνυ ἴσως μοχθηροῦ ἀνθρώπου καὶ φαύλου). In the *Apology* itself, when Socrates turns to address him at 24 B his first words are a sneer (πρὸς δὲ Μέλητον τὸν ἀγαθὸν καὶ φιλόπολιν, ὥς φησι), and at 26 E he declares, before he has made the point on which his declaration rests, that Meletus has

---

[1] In spite of Burnet's note I cannot doubt that ἐπίγρυπος is an unflattering epithet. *Rep.* 474 D, which he quotes, ridicules the practice of disguising physical shortcomings by flattering names. This is shown by the words (474 E) ὑποκοριζομένου τε καὶ εὐχερῶς φέροντος τὴν ὠχρότητα, ἐὰν ἐπὶ ὥρᾳ ᾖ.

instituted the prosecution 'in a spirit of youthful unprincipled insolence' (ὕβρει τινὶ καὶ ἀκολασίᾳ καὶ νεότητι).

As already remarked, Xenophon's *Apology* (§§ 19–21) also contains a short passage in which Socrates directly interrogates Meletus. Although I share the general scepticism as to the historical value of Xenophon's account, it seems to me not unlikely that in this particular he may have preserved a piece of real information: and it is on the strength of this agreement between Plato and Xenophon on the fact of *some* interrogation having occurred that I base the tentative suggestion, which I have been obliged to delay up to the present, regarding Plato's omission of that direct refutation of the corruption charge which, as I have explained, I am convinced Socrates must have offered.

In Xenophon's account Socrates challenges Meletus to mention any instances of persons corrupted by him, and suggests a number of possible sorts of corruption. To this Meletus replies, 'But I know of those whom you have persuaded to listen to you rather than to their parents'; this Socrates admits, and proceeds to justify or exculpate himself on this count. My inference is that Socrates did in fact deal with this, and with the other counts of the corruption charge, chiefly, if not exclusively, in the course of his interrogation of Meletus; but since Plato has chosen completely to transform the character of the interrogation, in such a way as to represent Meletus as having no idea of what he meant by 'corruption', he has made it impossible for himself, either in the interrogation section itself, or in any other part of the *Apology*, to reproduce the real refutation. In fact, this section has made it impossible for him to resume, in the third section, the same sort of 'substantial reproduction' which we have seen to be probably aimed at in the first. Fiction has imposed the necessity of further fiction. This result, which we have reached in a sense *a priori*, will be confirmed by an examination of the third section, to which I now turn.

The third section of the main speech (28 A– 35 D).

Socrates begins at 28 A by saying that he has made a sufficient reply to the charges of Meletus' indictment: his real danger comes not from these charges, but from 'the slander and ill-will of the multitude' (ἡ τῶν πολλῶν διαβολή τε καὶ φθόνος). Now in the first section that διαβολή had been traced to its source in the 'old accusers' and rebutted at considerable length; and at 24 B

Socrates had said that he had made a sufficient reply to the old accusers. Hence, both new and old accusers having been answered, we cannot regard this third section as constituting part of the formal ἀπολογία: as Burnet says, in form it is a digression. Now it would be quite natural for Socrates to have appended to his completed defence some account of his life and its significance to his fellow-citizens, if the defence proper had been restricted to the rebuttal of certain specific points made by the prosecution in substantiation of their indictment. But, in Plato's account, the defence proper had not taken any such narrow, restricted form: Socrates had fully explained the origin of his life's work in the oracle given to Chaerephon at Delphi, and had described his activity as an exposure of the false conceit of wisdom. The activity he had summed up at 23 B in these words, 'Hence it is that, in obedience to the god's command, I am still to-day going about examining and testing any citizen and any stranger that I fancy to be wise: and when I find that he is not, I show him that he is not, thus doing service to the god. And as the result of this occupation I have no leisure to engage in any of the state's affairs worth mentioning, or any domestic affairs either, but live in utter poverty owing to my service to the god'.

Now, the main topic of the third section, the digression, is again Socrates' divine mission: this is recognised by Burnet, who gives, as his title-summary of the section, 'The divine mission of Socrates'. But there is a well-marked difference between the earlier and the later account of the mission: in the earlier Socrates' activity is purely negative: he is purely ἐλεγχτικός and ἐξεταστικός; in the later, although he still speaks of himself as ἐξετάζων and ἐλέγχων, it is essentially positive: he is urging men to a sense of true values and to the care of the soul. The contrast comes out most clearly if we compare the sentences I have just quoted from 23 B with these at 30 A–B:

οὐδὲν γὰρ ἄλλο πράττων ἐγὼ περιέρχομαι ἢ πείθων ὑμῶν καὶ νεωτέρους καὶ πρεσβυτέρους μήτε σωμάτων ἐπιμελεῖσθαι μήτε χρημάτων πρότερον μηδὲ οὕτω σφόδρα ὡς τῆς ψυχῆς ὅπως ὡς ἀρίστη ἔσται, λέγων ὅτι οὐκ ἐκ χρημάτων ἀρετὴ γίγνεται, ἀλλ' ἐξ ἀρετῆς χρήματα καὶ τὰ ἄλλα ἀγαθὰ τοῖς ἀνθρώποις ἅπαντα καὶ ἰδίᾳ καὶ δημοσίᾳ.

These are of course not inconsistent, but complementary, accounts of Socrates' work.[1] But

[1] It is astonishing that Th. Gomperz (*Greek Thinkers*, II, p. 107), whose view of the general character of the *Apology* is thoroughly sound and moderate, should regard the account of Socrates' teaching given in the third section of the main speech

why should one appear in the formal defence, the other in the digression? We cannot but believe that the thing is done deliberately: and

as untrue to fact. His contention is that Plato has intentionally substituted the *effect* of Socrates' conversations for their actual purpose: they resulted in making men more virtuous, but they cannot have taken the form of direct exhortation to virtue, since that would have been inconsistent with Socrates' identification of virtue with knowledge; all that he aimed at was to rid men of intellectual error, to clear up their motives about the meaning of ethical terms.

This seems to me to imply a fundamental misunderstanding of Socrates' activity, the whole object of which was to substitute a true for a false standard of values. By examining their confused notions of the recognised virtues men would ultimately come to see that true morality is a rational system, a connected, coherent way of living, in which 'external goods' are only of value when rightly used. Gomperz's contention surely introduces just that sharp division between the intellect and the moral faculty which Socrates was insistent in denying: exhortation to 'practise virtue' or to 'care for the soul' was for Socrates identical with the search for knowledge, since the knowledge that he sought and would have others seek was the knowledge of the good life, the recognition of true values. And I do not see how this could be much better expressed than in the passage 29 D–30 B.

from a literary and artistic point of view it is admirable that an incomplete and quasi-negative portrait should be first given us. But is it likely that the arrangement is due to Socrates himself? Xenophon tells us, both in his *Apology* and his *Memorabilia*, that Socrates' speech was wholly unprepared, that he had deliberately made no preparation for his defence: and I can see no reason to reject this testimony. If we look more closely at the contexts of the two passages I have quoted, it is difficult to resist the conclusion that Plato is deliberately allowing us to see that the later passage is a re-handling, a fresh interpretation, of the earlier: the parallels of phraseology are not accidental, but designed: in the one place ἐπειδάν μοι μὴ δοκῇ (sc. σοφὸς εἶναι), in the other ἐάν μοι μὴ δοκῇ κεκτῆσθαι ἀρετήν: in both places a discrimination between ἀστοί and ξένοι: in both places the verb περιέρχομαι, in both places the verb ἐνδείκνυμαι, though in the later passage (29 D) it seems inappropriate (ἕωσπερ ἂν ἐμπνέω καὶ οἷός τε ὦ, οὐ μὴ παύσωμαι φιλοσοφῶν καὶ ὑμῖν παρακελευόμενός τε καὶ ἐνδεικνύμενος ὅτῳ ἂν ἀεὶ ἐντυγχάνω ὑμῶν)—for the participle has no complementary clause as it has in 23 B, ἐπειδάν μοι μὴ δοκῇ, τῷ θεῷ βοηθῶν ἐνδείκνυμαι ὅτι οὐκ ἔστι σοφός.

Nor are other indications lacking of this re-handling of previously used material, if we go further afield in comparing the two sections.

Again and again we find points repeated, but with a different bearing or from a different point of view: at 23 B, as we have seen, Socrates mentions the neglect of his personal affairs as due to his being fully occupied with the god's service: at 31 B he mentions it again, but now as *proof* that his work is imposed on him by God: οὐ γὰρ ἀνθρωπίνῳ ἔοικε τὸ ἐμὲ τῶν μὲν ἐμαυτοῦ πάντων ἠμεληκέναι καὶ ἀνέχεσθαι τῶν οἰκείων ἀμελουμένων τοσαῦτα ἤδη ἔτη. Near this, in both places, he mentions his poverty, in the earlier place as being the result of his λατρεία τοῦ θεοῦ, in the later as evidence that he takes no fee or reward. At 19 D he says that he does not instruct anyone (παιδεύειν), in order to distinguish himself from professional teachers like Gorgias and Prodicus: at 33 A he declares that he has never been the teacher (διδάσκαλος) of anybody, in order to rebut the imputation that he has made improper concessions (συγχωρήσας οὐδὲν παρὰ τὸ δίκαιον) to those supposed to be his disciples. At 19 D he says to the judges, 'Tell one another if you ever heard me holding conversations, long or short, about such (*i.e.* scientific) matters': at 30 B, after describing his hortatory discourses, he says, 'If anyone says that I speak of any subjects other than these, he is speaking falsely'. At 23 B he says he is continually going about examining and testing anyone he thinks may be wise: at 33 A, B it is

Socrates himself who is run after by others: he does not grudge anyone, young or old, rich or poor, who wants to hear him.

Everyone will remember that the general tone and attitude of Socrates in this third section is markedly different from that of the early part of the speech. There he was restrained, self-depreciatory, apologetic: here he is bold, self-laudatory, denunciatory. It is no doubt quite possible that such a change of tone did occur: nevertheless there are passages which one cannot help feeling to be Platonic encomium rather than Socratic self-appreciation. At 34 E, ἀλλ' οὖν δεδογμένον γέ ἐστι τὸν Σωκράτη διαφέρειν τῶν πολλῶν ἀνθρώπων. At 30 E, ἐὰν γάρ με ἀπο-κτείνητε, οὐ ῥᾳδίως ἄλλον τοιοῦτον εὑρήσετε, soon repeated at 31 A, τοιοῦτος οὖν ἄλλος οὐ ῥᾳδίως ὑμῖν γενήσεται. And there is too much insistence on Socrates' fearlessness of death: it is, I think, significant that the third section *opens* with this theme, drawing a parallel between Socrates and Achilles; after which comes a reference to his duty to stick to his post as he had stuck to it at Potidaea, Amphipolis, and Delium (οὗ ἐκεῖνοι ἔταττον ἔμενον ὥσπερ καὶ ἄλλος τις καὶ ἐκινδύνευον ἀποθανεῖν). At 30 B, 'Whether you acquit me or not, I will never do otherwise, οὐδ' εἰ μέλλω πολ-λάκις τεθνάναι'. At 32 B his attitude at the

Arginusae trial showed, he says, that he feared neither imprisonment nor death, and at 32 c, D, speaking of his defiance of the Thirty in the affair of Leon of Salamis he says τότε μέντοι ἐγὼ οὐ λόγῳ ἀλλ' ἔργῳ αὖ ἐνεδειξάμην ὅτι ἐμοὶ θανάτου μέλει οὐδ' ὁτιοῦν. We must of course make allowance for different conventions of reticence on such matters as between ourselves and fourth-century Greece: but, even so, this *motif* seems to me to be considerably more prominent than Socrates, as we know him elsewhere, would have made it.

I propose now to consider in some detail that part of this section which deals with Socrates' abstention from political activity, viz. 31 c–32 e.

Socrates' abstention from politics.

There is no good ground for doubting that Socrates did in fact at the trial refer to his abstention from political activity.[1] It must have been commonly remarked, and we may well believe that the prosecution had made some capital out of it. The *Apology* introduces the subject (31 c) as though they had not,[2] but we can infer

[1] As already observed, he refers to it in the first section of the main speech (23 B, οὔτε τι τῶν τῆς πόλεως πρᾶξαί μοι σχολὴ γέγονεν). A wholly different reason is now to be given.

[2] 31 C, ἴσως ἂν οὖν δόξειεν ἄτοπον εἶναι, κτλ.

nothing from this, since, as we have noticed, the Socrates of the *Apology* throughout makes hardly any reference to points of the accusers' speeches. That it was a matter which called for explanation can be seen from the reference made to it in Xenophon, *Mem.* 1, 6, § 15. Nor need we doubt that Socrates alleged his Divine Sign as restraining him in this matter: at all events the same reason is alleged in *Rep.* 496 c. But what follows in the *Apology*, viz. 31 D–32 D, is less possible to accept as a reproduction in substance of what Socrates may have said.

He begins by rationalising the Sign, that is to say he explains why the restraint which it imposed commended itself to his reason. This is not in itself unlikely, indeed it was only to be expected that Socrates should have sought for a reason: and we get a similar procedure at 40 B. But the reason which he finds is remarkable: if he had attempted a political career, he would have perished long ago and done no service either to himself or to Athens. οὐ γὰρ ἔστιν ὅστις ἀνθρώπων σωθήσεται οὔτε ὑμῖν οὔτε ἄλλῳ πλήθει οὐδενὶ γνησίως ἐναντιούμενος καὶ διακωλύων πολλὰ ἄδικα καὶ παράνομα ἐν τῇ πόλει γίγνεσθαι, ἀλλ' ἀναγκαῖόν ἐστι τὸν τῷ ὄντι μαχούμενον ὑπὲρ τοῦ δικαίου, καὶ εἰ μέλλει ὀλίγον χρόνον σωθήσεσθαι, ἰδιωτεύειν ἀλλὰ μὴ δημοσιεύειν. 'In this impressive sentence', says James Adam, 'Plato appears definitely to renounce his early aspirations after political life': and Adam is duly trounced by Burnet for absurdly confusing Plato with Socrates. Nevertheless, I believe his instinct was right. The sentiment implies an extreme opposition to democracy which it is difficult to imagine as having been adopted by Socrates in the decade 450–440, when this decision must have been made. Was the early Periclean regime likely to have appeared to him in this light? Was it true that then every honest critic of the Athenian assembly went in danger of losing his life? And did Socrates really think that anyone with honourable political ambitions, anyone who 'meant to fight for the right' must keep clear of politics? Xenophon at least did not so conceive him, for his Socrates urges[1] the diffident Charmides to enter politics. The period which these words seem to fit, the era of judicial murders and political assassinations, dawned only with the Revolution of 411, when, it is pertinent to remark, Plato was just emerging from childhood. In that year the restored democracy executed Antiphon and Archeptolemus for high treason, and the bones of Phrynichus were cast beyond the frontier. That Plato's family and their friends

[1] *Mem.* III, vii.

sympathised with the programme of these men—
at all events with their original programme—
that they regarded them as 'sincere opponents
of the multitude' and as 'fighting for the right'
cannot be doubted, although it is probable that
when the split in the oligarchical party developed
their sympathies went with Theramenes and
Critias. But the Plato who wrote these lines was
thinking less of 411 than of the 'democratic
terror', as Mr Ferguson[1] terms it, of 410–405.
For in these years it was literally true that anyone who ventured to oppose the democracy went
in danger of his life. 'A set of acrid politicians
and sycophants...encompassed the exile, dis-
franchisement, or judicial murder of many persons. Others they blackmailed by threats of indictment.'[2] It was in these years that Plato
formed his lifelong hatred of democracy. Mr
Ferguson is surely right when he says that in the
famous passage, *Republic*, 496 B–D, Plato writes
with the Athens of these years in his mind,
though I think we should add, on the evidence
of his seventh *Epistle*, that the passage also reflects the deepening of his convictions in the
years which immediately followed 399. Now if
we compare the present passage of the *Apology*

[1] *C.A.H.* v, p. 349, heading.
[2] Ferguson, *ibid.* p. 351.

natural inference, that this first picture is really that of Plato again, is confirmed by a later passage of the same Epistle. At 330 D–331 D he has occasion to speak of the conditions which make it right and proper for a man to decline to help his fellow-citizens with advice and counsel, that is to abstain from political activity. 'When men are travelling altogether outside the path of right government and flatly refuse to move in the right path, and start by giving notice to their adviser that he must leave the government alone and make no change in it under penalty of death —if such men should order their counsellors to pander to their wishes and desires and to advise them in what way their object may most readily and easily be once for all accomplished, I should consider as unmanly one who accepts the duty of giving such forms of advice, and one who refuses it to be a true man.'[1] And a little further on: 'The wise man should go through life with the same attitude of mind towards his country. If she should appear to him to be following a policy which is not a good one, he should say so, provided that his words are not likely either to fall on deaf ears or to lead to the loss of his own life'.[2] These passages have surely the ring of

[1] 330 E–331 A, tr. Harward.

[2] 331 C–D.

personal experience. Even clearer is a passage in the fifth *Epistle*, where Plato goes out of his way to defend his own abstention from Athenian politics: addressing an imaginary critic he says, 'Plato was born late in his country's history, and found the democracy grown old and accustomed by his predecessors to many forms of action quite different from what he would advise. For nothing would have pleased him more than to have offered advice to the people as to a father, if he had not believed that he would have been running useless risks where there was no prospect of doing good'.[1]

It will be observed that all these three passages, like that of the *Apology* which we are considering, refer to the danger incurred by one who would embark on political life. It is impossible to doubt that Plato did feel that for him a political career would have meant flinging away his life uselessly. It was Plato, not Socrates, for whom this danger was real; for it was Plato who declared that the salvation of society depended on that radical revolution in political and social life which he sums up in *Ep.* VII, 326 A–B, in the words: 'There will be no cessation of evils for the sons of men, till either those who are pursuing a right and true philosophy receive sovereign power in the States, or those in power in the

[1] 322 B, tr. Harward.

States by some dispensation of providence become true philosophers'.[1]

And further, although there would have been nothing dishonourable in Socrates' decision to abstain from politics, any more than there was in Plato's, if he had based it on this ground, yet it is surely unlike the Socrates pictured in the very next page (*Apology*, 32) as utterly regardless of death and danger: consider especially 32 D, ἐμοὶ θανάτου μὲν μέλει, εἰ μὴ ἀγροικότερον ἦν εἰπεῖν, οὐδ' ὁτιοῦν, τοῦ δὲ μηδὲν ἄδικον μηδ' ἀνόσιον ἐργάζεσθαι, τούτου δὲ τὸ πᾶν μέλει.

My conclusion is that Plato is here reconstructing Socrates on the basis of his own experience of Athenian politics. He is not deliberately substituting himself, but genuinely believes that the considerations which determined his own career had, in this matter, also determined that of Socrates. In doing this he has been oblivious of the difference between the Athens of the middle fifth century and that of 410–390: he has in his description of Socrates as πλήθει ἐναντιούμενος suggested a greater degree of anti-democratic sentiment than Socrates actually possessed,[2] and

---

[1] tr. Harward.

[2] It is not to be doubted that thorough-going opposition to a democratic constitution would have been fatal to its advocate, even in the days of Pericles.

he has attributed to him an attitude of cautious expediency which is hardly in keeping with the rest of the portrait drawn in these later pages of the third section of the main speech.

Why did Socrates in fact abstain from politics? Probably because he knew that his gift lay in the power of influencing individuals by conversing with them, and that he had no power of swaying large gatherings. Doubtless he thought, too, that the former is a more valuable gift than the latter.[1] I see no reason to doubt that what Xenophon makes him say to Antiphon in *Mem.* 1, 6, § 15, is in substance correct: 'Should I play a more important part in politics by engaging in them alone, or by setting myself to turn out as many adequate politicians as possible?' By adequate politicians (τὰ πολιτικὰ ἱκανοὺς πράττειν) Socrates meant good men.

We must now turn to the evidence (τεκμήρια) by which Plato's Socrates substantiates his assertion that the honest critic of the people, who means to fight for the right, must remain in a private station if he is not to perish. The evidence consists in Socrates' experience first at the trial of the generals after Arginusae, and secondly in the affair of Leon of Salamis. It may be admitted

[1] This is what the explanation given in 23 B really amounts to.

that the first is a good instance, in so far as he did then endanger his life; though it seems to have been a very exceptional occasion, when the Assembly was worked up to a pitch of fury and mob passion unparalleled in Athenian history.[1] And in this first instance the danger did arise from the fact that Socrates occupied a public position, as one of the prytanies. But in the second instance he did not occupy any public position, so that this does not in fact substantiate his assertion in the least. Moreover the account of these τεκμήρια seems to reveal a second motive for its insertion, namely to show (in both instances) that Socrates did not fear death, and would not compromise with his conscience in order to avoid it: 32 A, ἀκούσατε δή μοι τὰ συμβεβηκότα, ἵνα εἰδῆτε ὅτι οὐδ' ἂν ἑνὶ ὑπεικάθοιμι παρὰ τὸ δίκαιον δείσας θάνατον: 32 C, τότε μέντοι ἐγὼ οὐ λόγῳ ἀλλ' ἔργῳ αὖ ἐνεδειξάμην ὅτι ἐμοὶ θανάτου μὲν μέλει...οὐδ' ὁτιοῦν, τοῦ δὲ μηδὲν ἄδικον μηδ' ἀνόσιον ἐργάζεσθαι, τούτου δὲ τὸ πᾶν μέλει. The inference which suggests itself is that Plato's original motive in mentioning the two cases of Socrates' fearless behaviour was the motive expressed in these two passages, and that the

[1] Cf. Grote-Mitchell-Caspari, *History of Greece*, p. 760, 'This temporary burst of wrong...so foreign to the habitual character of the people'.

notion of making them τεκμήρια of the principle announced at 31 E–32 A was an afterthought. It is very improbable that Socrates, if he himself referred to the two affairs at all, used them for these two quite distinct ends.

To recapitulate: the third section of the main speech has been found to exhibit some remarkable features: a deliberate, conscious, doubling or re-handling of topics belonging to the first section, a recurrent tone of self-laudation unnatural to Socrates, and an explanation of Socrates' abstention from political life which is in fact a projection of the writer's own experience. In what way can we reasonably account for all this?

The answer is, in my judgment, that Plato with consummate skill has converted a self-imposed difficulty into a magnificent opportunity. The necessity for omitting Socrates' actual reply to the διαφθορά charge, a necessity arising in the way that I have suggested, had made Plato bring his work to an apparent 'full close'[1] at 28 A, B. Yet he must have felt, as soon as he had written these words, that the full significance

---

[1] The close is impressive in its brevity and simplicity: καὶ τοῦτ᾽ ἔστιν ὃ ἐμὲ αἱρεῖ, ἐάνπερ αἱρῇ, οὐ Μέλητος οὐδὲ Ἄνυτος ἀλλ᾽ ἡ τῶν πολλῶν διαβολή τε καὶ φθόνος. ἃ δὴ πολλοὺς καὶ ἄλλους καὶ ἀγαθοὺς ἄνδρας ᾕρηκεν, οἶμαι δὲ καὶ αἱρήσει· οὐδὲν δὲ δεινὸν μὴ ἐν ἐμοὶ στῇ.

of Socrates' life and work had been by no means
brought out in what he had written. And as he
reflected and went over his memory of the trial,
it is not unlikely that he grew increasingly convinced that the actual speech was itself inadequate
to fulfil the real purpose which he had in view,
namely the presentation of Socrates as he saw
him. I do not suppose Plato to have had in his
mind, before he began the composition of the
Apology, any clear notion of how far he would
permit himself invention: but I should conjecture
that the temptation—if that is the right word—
or the urge to invention grew upon him as he
proceeded with the work: so that when, with
the 'full close' of 28 A, B he found himself faced
with the alternatives of further invention or
silence, he embraced the former without compunction. He decided to make Socrates say what
he, Plato, felt, retaining however just enough of
the form of ἀπολογία to meet the minimum demands of verisimilitude.

It would be an unnecessary impertinence for
us to seek to excuse Plato for doing this. The
complete success of his experiment, whereby the
figure of Socrates is made to live for all time
thanks to an eloquence and an art comparable to
that of the *Phaedo* and the *Symposium*, makes
criticism petty and irrelevant. To us the experi-

ment seems daring: to his age with its quicker perceptions, with its habituation to the dramatic revelation of character through the spoken word, with its almost total ignorance of the objective analysis of character familiar to ourselves in historical and biographical writing, it would seem wholly natural. Plato's contemporaries would know instinctively what he was doing.

Of course we need not rule out the possibility —it is indeed a probability—that the third section reflects certain things which Socrates said. In particular I think it likely that there is one such passage at 30 E 3–31 A 5, where Socrates, comparing himself to a gadfly, says that the Athenians are likely to put him to death because of their irritation at being roused out of their drowsy inertia by the stings he implants in them. My inference is based on certain passages in the *Gorgias*, which have some importance in connexion with the whole question of Socrates' defence, and which have been discussed by H. Gomperz in the paper previously referred to.

At 522 B, C Socrates says that if anybody should bring him before a law-court because he rebukes the Athenians with hard words, he would find himself in the greatest embarrassment: he could not tell them the truth, namely that he had done so in the interests of the

Athenians themselves, without setting his judges against him; and so no way of defence remained to him (οὔτε τὸ ἀληθὲς ἔξω εἰπεῖν, ὅτι δικαίως πάντα ταῦτα ἐγὼ λέγω, καὶ πράττω τὸ ὑμέτερον δὴ τοῦτο, ὦ ἄνδρες δικασταί, οὔτε ἄλλο οὐδέν· ὥστε ἴσως, ὅτι ἂν τύχω, τοῦτο πείσομαι). At 486 A, B Callicles tells Socrates that if he were to be arrested on a criminal charge of which he was innocent he would not know what to do, but would grow dizzy and gape and have nothing to say: and at 527 A Socrates retorts on Callicles that when Callicles stands at the bar of Rhadamanthus he will do likewise (χασμήσει καὶ ἰλιγγιάσεις οὐδὲν ἧττον ἢ ἐγὼ ἐνθάδε σὺ ἐκεῖ). From the first-quoted passage (522 B, C) Gomperz infers that the *Apology* must be later than the *Gorgias*, that it cannot indeed even have been planned when the *Gorgias* was written: for Socrates there does precisely what, in the *Gorgias*, he says he will not be able to do. The other two passages suggest to Gomperz the possibility (he expresses himself tentatively) that Socrates made no formal speech in his defence at all. I will not discuss these suggestions, both of which seem utterly impossible. But what inferences should be drawn? With regard to Socrates' 'dizziness and gaping' I would say that no inference need be drawn, nor can be drawn: for Socrates' endorsement of

Callicles' suggestion is only apparent: in effect he says, 'You think I shall be embarrassed when I am put on my trial in a human law-court: I can tell you that it is you who will be embarrassed at the last judgment'. But the passage 522 B, C cannot be so easily dismissed; and if rightly understood it throws some light on the nature of Socrates' defence on the charge of διαφθορὰ τῶν νέων. The key to the whole passage 521 E– 522 E is to be found in what Socrates says about the true βοήθεια at 522 D. Plato wants to bring out the point that, although Socrates was (or, adapting the tense to the prophecy, would be) in the ordinary sense ἀδύνατος ἑαυτῷ βοηθεῖν, yet he had (would have) the only 'support' that matters in the final account, the support of his own conscience as one μήτε περὶ ἀνθρώπους μήτε περὶ θεοὺς ἄδικον μηδὲν μήτε εἰρηκὼς μήτε εἰργα- σμένος. When Socrates forecasts his helplessness in the law-court, we are meant to understand, not that he will in fact refrain from telling his judges, the representatives of his fellow-countrymen, the truth about themselves and his mission to them, but that there will be available to him no βοήθεια in the sense that Callicles and everybody else thinks of a defendant's βοήθεια against the charge on which he is arraigned. In the eyes of the world Socrates, accused of corrupting the young, is the helpless fool who cannot defend himself. In other words, when he says οὔτε τὸ ἀληθὲς ἔξω εἰπεῖν...οὔτε ἄλλο οὐδέν, he is deliberately adopting the standpoint of Callicles, who cannot conceive of a defendant doing anything except muster arguments for a favourable verdict. This admirably subtle example of Socratic irony prepares the way for Callicles' expression of contemptuous pity at 522 c, and consequently for the description of the true βοήθεια.

A hint is furnished to the understanding reader by Socrates' earlier words in 522 A, ἢ εἰ εἴποι τὴν ἀλήθειαν, ὅτι ταῦτα πάντα ἐγὼ ἐποίουν ὑγιεινῶς, ὁπόσον οἴει ἂν ἀναβοῆσαι τοὺς τοιούτους δικαστάς; for if he knows Socrates at all he will not suppose that he would be deterred from telling people the truth just because they are likely to raise an uproar.

It should be incidentally observed that there is no reference here to the charge of irreligion, in either of its parts; there is no suggestion that Socrates will not be able to defend himself on *that* charge in the ordinary way, by denying it and substantiating his denial. In regard to the corruption charge, the *Gorgias* passage—far from being, as Gomperz thinks, inconsistent with the *Apology*—is really quite compatible with it, and helps us to reconstruct Socrates' own defence. In discussing the meaning of the corruption charge I have argued that what the prosecution emphasised was the pernicious moral effects resulting from the ἀπορία to which Socrates reduces his listeners. Socrates' reply was, in effect, 'Yes, I do reduce them to ἀπορία, I do taunt them[1] with intellectual and moral sloth, and that is just what they need; though I know that it is what you all resent, so that you will have little compunction in condemning me to death'. The *Gorgias*, with the irony which I have explained, makes Socrates say that he will be afraid to take this line; the *Apology*, in the passage under discussion, preserves an echo of Socrates' reply incorporated (as I believe) in a setting of Plato's own fabrication.

[1] ὀνειδίζων, 30 E 7: cf. ὀνειδιῶ, 30 A 1.

CHAPTER VI

THE SECOND AND THIRD SPEECHES
AND THE TOTAL PICTURE
OF SOCRATES

Of the second speech (the ἀντιτίμησις) and the third I have little to say, except that they seem to me much closer to reality than the section we have been considering. That Socrates did claim as his due σίτησις ἐν τῷ πρυτανείῳ I regard as beyond doubt. I do not indeed agree with Wilamowitz's argument, that it would have been harmful to Socrates' reputation for Plato to have fathered the claim on him; but the decisive considerations are:

(1) The increase in the adverse vote: Diogenes Laertius says that eighty more judges voted for the death-penalty than had voted Socrates guilty. Now Plato says nothing about this increased vote; if he had invented the σίτησις claim he would in all probability have sought to make it more plausible by mentioning the increase, and connecting it with the claim. He could easily have found an opportunity for this in the third speech: and the mere fact that the third speech has no reference to the claim, and that it appears *only* in the second speech, is in favour of its being historical. Plato did not need

to tell his readers that the hostile majority had increased: they knew it and they knew its reason.

(2) The account in Diogenes (II, 41–2) mentions the claim, but reverses the order of the proceedings: the money fine (100 drachmae or a mina) was first proposed by Socrates, and when this caused an uproar the claim of maintenance in the Prytaneum was substituted. The biographer does not mention his authority here; but the point is that his account is plainly independent of Plato, not only in the reversal of the order of the claims, but in the omission to mention the offer by Plato and other friends to guarantee a payment of thirty minae. We have therefore confirmation of the σίτησις claim by an account independent of the *Apology*.

I am inclined to agree with Burnet (on 36 D) that this claim 'is the μεγαληγορία which puzzled Xenophon': or rather it was principally this, for we may suppose that Socrates' scornful refusal to appeal for pity on the conventional lines, to produce his children, etc., was also in Xenophon's mind. It may seem curious that Xenophon does not mention the σίτησις claim, either in his *Apology* or his *Memorabilia*, though there were obvious opportunities for doing so at § 21 and § 23 of the former work. The reason I would suggest is that this particular instance of μεγαληγορία either seemed so incredible that he shrank from mentioning it, or else that he was shocked by what he thought misplaced levity. It is, I think, quite possible for a man like Xenophon to have concealed in his defence of Socrates the very thing which he really thought needed defending. To pit his silence against the testimony of Plato would be very foolish.

Further, it is not unlikely that Socrates justified his claim to free maintenance in the sort of way that Plato represents. The only part of this second speech which raises doubts is 36 B–C, where we get a repetition of the previous explanation of Socrates' abstention from politics, expressed this time in a sentence peculiarly offensive to modern ears at least (ἡγησάμενος ἐμαυτὸν τῷ ὄντι ἐπιεικέστερον εἶναι ἢ ὥστε εἰς ταῦτ' ἰόντα σῴζεσθαι), followed by a repetition of the *positive* side of his mission in terms very similar to those used at 30 A–B.

The ultimate proposal of a fine of thirty minae, made at the request of Socrates' friends, including Plato himself, is obviously historical, and I will not waste time in defending it. I have already discussed[1] Xenophon's counter-state-

---

[1] Pp. 15 f. *supra*. The statement in question does not imply Xenophon's disbelief in the σίτησις claim, which was not a real ἀντιτίμησις.

ment, suggesting that it arose from deliberate suppression in his authority or authorities; the same reason must, I suppose, account for the omission of the final proposal by Diogenes Laertius. The biographer, although he cites Plato's *Apology* in § 39 discards it, *more suo*, in favour of Justus of Tiberias and Eubulides in §§ 41–2: he would be rash who sought to explain this writer's predilections with confidence, but probably he thought that the last lines of 38 B showed Socrates as weak and inconsistent, and were therefore untrue; unless indeed they escaped his notice, or his memory, altogether.

To turn finally to the third speech, I agree with Burnet's contention (in his introductory note to this speech) that there is no ground for supposing that Socrates would not have been allowed to make it. I would add that those who have thought otherwise (and Wilamowitz[1] is their protagonist) seem to attribute to Plato an utter lack of dramatic realism. If it was (as they imply) a hard-and-fast rule of Athenian courts that no defendant should speak after sentence, it was surely impossible for Plato to have represented Socrates as doing so, even if the whole of the *Apology* from the first word to the last were sheer invention. Equally groundless is Wilamo-

[1] *Platon*, I, p. 165.

witz's assertion that the judges would not have
stayed to listen: curiosity, if nothing else, would
have induced many to linger.[1] There is perhaps
more substance in the contention[2] of Schanz that
they would not have listened to a philosophical
disquisition, or in that of Ivo Bruns,[3] that Socrates could not have delivered a long harangue
on the life after death. To both these contentions
however it seems a sufficient answer that Socrates
was Socrates, and that deductions or assumptions
which might carry weight in ordinary cases carry
none in this.

Nevertheless, if I have been right in detecting
encomium as prominent in the latter part of the
first speech, and traceable in the second, it is *a
priori* likely that Plato would not have refrained
from it in this final speech. We find it, I think,
in 38 D–E where we get yet another reference to
the refusal to appeal for pity, and to Socrates'
fearlessness of death. We may notice that this
latter *motif* is now used not, as previously
(37 C ff.), to point the contrast between Socrates'
death and a continued life that would have been
a worse alternative for him, but to contrast
his own better fate with the worse fate of his

[1] Cf. Horneffer's sensible remarks, *op. cit.* pp.
129–30.

[2] *Op. cit.* p. 74.   [3] *Op. cit.* p. 210.

accusers (39 A–B). While I would not contend that Socrates may not have arranged his topics in this way, yet I think it more likely that we owe to Plato's literary skill this 'partition of antitheses', if I may so style it, between the second and third speeches.

At the beginning of the speech (38 c) the suggestion that Athens will be abused for executing Socrates reads like a prophecy after the event. The words must, I think, refer to criticism outside Athens: and it does not seem probable that Socrates, who had hardly ever quitted the city except on military service, and who had only formed personal connexions with a few non-Athenians, should suppose that his execution would attract such notice elsewhere as to bring odium upon his city. The presence of a number of his followers at Megara, after his death, would have been likely to spread his fame abroad and bring discredit upon Athens, who was never loved by her neighbour.

In his address to those judges who had voted against him, Socrates says that they must not expect that by his death they will have freed themselves from criticism and censure: 'You will find that you have more critics, whom up to the present I have restrained, though you did not realise it; and the younger they are the more troublesome they will be, and the more you will resent them' (39 C–D). Grote argues that the non-fulfilment of this prophecy attests its genuineness; Valgimigli, on the other hand, thinks that this argument will not hold, since 'the prophecy is quite vague and indeterminate, and since Plato himself, thinking of himself and his fellow-Socratics, might have considered such a prophecy as already fulfilled, or at least soon about to find fulfilment'.[1] The fact is that we know so little about the activities of Socrates' followers after his death that it is impossible to say whether any of them did attempt to carry on his work in his own fashion. That literary productions are hinted at seems to me most unlikely: least of all can any of Plato's own dialogues have been in his mind. Indeed I can find nothing decisive on either side: the words may quite well have been uttered by Socrates, or they may quite well have been written by Plato in view of occurrences between 399 and 393. But what needs pointing out is that they involve a contradiction of what was said at 31 A. There Socrates, after describing himself as the gadfly that is ceaselessly stinging the people of Athens out of their slumbers—ἐγείρων καὶ πείθων καὶ ὀνειδίζων—adds: 'You will not easily find another like me...but are

[1] *Op. cit.* pp. 35–6.

likely to go on sleeping for the rest of your lives, unless God in his kindness should send you another'. What are we to make of this contradiction? One possibility of course is that Socrates said neither thing: that possibility obviously cannot be disproved; but if we have to choose between them, the preference I think clearly belongs to 39 D, since 31 A belongs to that part of the whole *Apology* where the most exalted claims are made for Socrates, and where we have most reason to believe that he is not speaking.[1] Again, at 23 C Socrates is speaking of the young men who imitate his ἐξέτασις of the wise: this seems in partial contradiction of both the other passages: of 31 A since there *are* followers to carry on the ἐξέτασις, and of 39 D since they were not kept in check during Socrates' lifetime. But it seems easier to reconcile 23 C with 39 D than with 31 A: for the words οὓς νῦν ἐγὼ κατεῖχον at 39 D need mean no more than that Socrates had restrained the excessive zeal of his followers, without silencing them altogether: whereas 31 A would naturally suggest, taken by itself, that he had no associates in his ἐξέτασις

[1] This belief is not really inconsistent with my suggestion above (pp. 130 ff.) that this very passage incorporates an echo of Socrates' defence on the corruption charge.

at all. It is to be noticed that this suggestion of Socrates' followers as mere bystanders at his talks comes out again at 33 c. Putting these considerations together we may infer that 23 c and 39 d give the true account, viz. that Socrates had associates who pursued his own characteristic procedure, both of 'elenchus' and of 'protreptic', while 31 a and 33 c reflect the view of Plato who was not one of these 'active' associates, and who tended to think of Socrates as an isolated figure whose work would end with his death.

At the very end of the speech it is somewhat surprising to find Socrates once again addressing the hostile judges, or rather (to be exact) announcing to the friendly judges a request that he has to make of the others. He begs that they will take their revenge for all the annoyance that he has caused them by practising his own methods on his sons if, when they grow up, they neglect the quest of virtue, and imagine they are worth something when they are not.

The passage may perhaps be regarded as a characteristic piece of whimsical Socratic banter: Socrates can hardly have imagined that these men would be likely to adopt the course recommended for 'getting their own back' on him. But if Socrates really said this, why did he not say it earlier when directly addressing the hostile judges? I think it more likely to be an afterthought of Platonic invention, reflecting the situation at the date of composition of the *Apology*. Of the three sons, Lamprocles was in 399 a μειρά-κιον, Sophroniscus and Menexenus were παιδία (34 D), the last-named being apparently a baby in arms (*Phaedo*, 60 A). By the time the *Apology* came to be written Lamprocles had grown into a young man, possibly Sophroniscus also. Aristotle (*Rhetoric*, 1390, B 30) says of the sons, without distinction, that they displayed stupidity (ἀβελτερία) and sluggishness (νωθρότης). Had Plato, and perhaps other Socratics, hoped that they would prove true sons of their father, and is he here writing with a feeling of bitter disappointment? So perhaps we may best account for this somewhat unfortunate passage.

And then—ἀλλὰ γὰρ ἤδη ὥρα ἀπιέναι. It may be thought characteristic of Socrates that he should use a phrase suggestive rather of the close of a social evening than of a passage to the condemned cell. Perhaps it was, and in any case it would be ridiculous to base on such a trifle our judgment on the nature of the third speech. Nevertheless it is perhaps worth comparing *Protagoras*, 361 E, νῦν δ' ὥρα ἤδη καὶ ἐπ' ἄλλο τι τρέπεσθαι; *Meno*, 100 B, νῦν δ' ἐμοὶ μὲν ὥρα ποι ἰέναι; *Euthyphro*, 15 E (Euth. *loquitur*), νῦν γὰρ σπεύδω ποι, καί μοι ὥρα ἀπιέναι; *Theaet*. 210 D, νῦν μὲν οὖν ἀπαντητέον μοι εἰς τὴν τοῦ βασιλέως στοάν. The use here of the same sort of closing formula as comes naturally in a fictitious dialogue suggests that the line drawn in Plato's mind between the present work and the Σωκρατικοὶ λόγοι, which had already made their appearances as a literary form, was not quite so hard and fast as some writers have supposed.[1]

It would be unsatisfactory to conclude this study of the structure of the *Apology* without some consideration of the important question whether the picture of Socrates which it presents to us is substantially true in the sense of being a complete picture. Has Plato, whether giving us Socrates' defence or his own defence of Socrates, told us all that Socrates really stood for, all his significance for his own age and for posterity? Or has he selected, and left much out: and if so are the omissions legitimate, or do they involve a falsification of the picture? What of the philosopher who held the theory of Forms (Ideas), and deduced therefrom his belief in the immortality of the human soul? What of the

[1] The *Euthyphro* passage in particular should, I think, carry some weight if, as I believe with Ritter, it was already written.

young Socrates who knew all about the scientific speculation of his day, and the middle-aged Socrates who lived with his disciples in a thinking-shop? What was he *before* Chaerephon consulted the oracle, and why did Chaerephon put his question?

An adequate answer to these questions would no doubt involve a thoroughgoing examination of the Socrates-problem in all its aspects. The identity of the Platonic with the real Socrates, has, as everyone knows, been maintained with a great wealth of learning and skilled argument by Burnet and Taylor. I have not the ambition to examine their thesis as a whole: much has been said on the other side, perhaps most cogently and exhaustively by Léon Robin in *Revue des Études grecques* xxix (1916), pp. 129–65.

But I am at least bound to consider the Socrates-problem in so far as the credibility of the *Apology* is affected, the more so since the evidence of the *Apology* has not, in my judgment, received anything like its due consideration. My own belief is that the Socrates of the *Apology* is true to life, and that any evidence which conflicts with it must be rejected. The evidence of *Apology*, 18 A–19 D, where Socrates is defending himself against his 'old accusers', *i.e.* against misrepresentations of long-standing, is, I will say roundly, utterly and entirely irreconcilable with the picture of Socrates in the *Clouds*. In substantiating this assertion, it is simpler and more natural to begin by asking what evidence, if any, confirms the general features of Aristophanes' picture, in particular the figure of Socrates as head of a φροντιστήριον. Now there is no reason to doubt that Socrates in his early days (about 450 B.C. or earlier) came into contact with Archelaus, who expounded the philosophy of Anaxagoras in Athens, and that he attended his lectures; but that he devoted himself to scientific experiment or research, above all that he succeeded Archelaus as head of a scientific school, is impossible to believe. For in that case the representation of him in popular talk and on the comic stage as τά τε μετέωρα φροντιστὴς καὶ τὰ ὑπὸ γῆς πάντα ἀνεζητηκώς would not have been ψευδῆ κατηγορημένα (18 A) and διαβολή (19 A), but the truth. It is not the least use to say that Socrates had dropped these pursuits when he found science unsatisfying, or discovered that he had no gift for it: for the language which he uses rules out (assuming him to be speaking truthfully and not misleadingly) the possibility that at any age whatever he engaged in scientific speculation or research. At 19 D he challenges any of his judges to assert that he had heard Socrates uttering a

single word about such matters; amongst the
judges there must have been at least some contemporaries of his own, who could have called
his bluff, if it was a bluff. It is impossible to
believe Burnet's assertion (in his note on 19 c 4)
that Socrates' disclaimer of all understanding of
natural science is ironical. 'The ἑταῖρος of Archelaus', he says, 'must have known all there was
to be known about such things, only it did not
seem to him to be knowledge.' If Socrates did
know all there was to be known about such
things, he is not being ironical, but is lying, and
that too to save his own skin, to influence the
court in his favour: for the rebuttal of the old
accusers' charge of μετεωροσοφία is designed
to remove the popular misconceptions which he
feels to be the real present danger. With reference to the challenge just mentioned, Burnet
says 'the attitude of Socrates being such as is
described here and at greater length in the
Phaedo [*sic*], we may be sure that he never talked
about these matters in public'. The last two
words conceal an implicit *suggestio falsi*, for Socrates makes no distinction between what he
said in public and what he said in private: indeed
in a later passage (33 B) he says, 'If anyone declares that he has ever learnt or heard from me
in private anything beyond what everyone else

has heard, you may be sure that he is not telling the truth'. Nor can we have recourse to the supposition that Plato is exaggerating the detachment of Socrates from scientific studies: for it is not a question of emphasis or phraseology, of the exact content of particular sentences, but of the whole substance of Socrates' defence against the 'old accusers'; and who will venture to assert that that is all fathered upon Socrates by Plato? Least of all can I understand how scholars who hold that the *Apology* is a close reproduction of Socrates' actual speech at the same time defend the caricature of the *Clouds* as a fair caricature. What reason is there to doubt that Aristophanes did what Socrates says he did, namely accepted the misrepresentation of him already in favour with the man in the street? Socrates makes it clear that, in his view, the comic dramatists did not *invent* Σωκράτης μετεωροσοφιστής: 18 c, ὃ δὲ πάντων ἀλογώτατον, ὅτι οὐδὲ τὰ ὀνόματα οἷόν τε αὐτῶν εἰδέναι καὶ εἰπεῖν, πλὴν εἴ τις κωμῳδοποιὸς τυγχάνει ὤν. And when he turns to explain the origin of the misrepresentation, he finds it in the irritation felt by the victims of Socratic dialectic; speaking (at 23 c–d) of the young men who imitated his own method of 'examining' those reputed to be wise he says, 'Consequently those who are examined by them become angry with me,

instead of with themselves, and say that Socrates
is a detestable fellow who corrupts the young: and
when they are asked what he does or what he
teaches that corrupts them, they don't know and
can't say: but in order to avoid looking foolish
they use expressions that are the stock criticisms
levelled at all philosophers, and talk about "things
in the heaven and things under the earth" and
"disbelief in the gods" and "making the weaker
case the stronger"'. What could be plainer?
Socrates, because he was a φιλόσοφος in his own
special sense, suffered from the attacks and libels
directed against philosophers and scientists in
general. Aristophanes, who certainly believed
that Socrates was, like Euripides, a mischievous
meddler with sound traditional standards of conduct, joyfully adapted these attacks and libels to
the comic stage. And it was just because the man
in the street was so magnificently indiscriminating
in his detestation of 'philosophers' that Aristophanes could get across with his hotch-potch
figure, his amalgam of Ionian scientist, ascetic
Orphic devotee, hair-splitting quibbler, professor
of grammar, and unscrupulous advocate. He was
not attacking a type nor the 'Sophistic move-
ment': he was attacking Socrates, in whom he
saw, or pretended to see, everything he detested
exemplified at its worst: Socrates felt the attack

as personal, and as seriously meant: otherwise he would not have made particular reference to the *Clouds*: and if Plato pictures him on terms of friendly intercourse with Aristophanes at Agathon's symposium some half-dozen years afterwards, this is best explained by supposing that Socrates was tolerant enough to feel no resentment against the poet who had only given expression to what so many thought.[1]

'If Sokrates did not, in fact, preside over such a society (*sc.* as that of the φροντιστήριον) are we', asks Burnet,[2] 'to suppose that Aristophanes himself invented the idea of a scientific school, or that he knew of those in other cities by hearsay and transferred them in imagination to Athens?' For myself, I find it quite easy to suppose either of these things: after all what was a 'scientific school' but a house where a number of people came together for instruction and provided themselves with some rudimentary appara-

---

[1] At 18 D Aristophanes should be understood as included amongst οἱ αὐτοὶ πεπεισμένοι ἄλλους πείθοντες, who are distinguished from the malicious attackers. It may be added that the *Symposium* could hardly have been written by one who had himself *invented* the passages referring to Aristophanes in the *Apology*.

[2] *Greek Philosophy*, Part I, p. 147.

tus, globes, diagrams and so forth? If Socrates was to be shown on the stage as a mischievous teacher, he had to be seen with his pupils: the scene of his teaching had to be a local habitation, and to have a name. But in point of fact there is no need to attribute to Aristophanes this daring flight of fanciful invention, or this transference to Athens of such a remarkable foreign phenomenon. Professor Burnet has himself suggested, in the previous sentence, that Archelaus may have established such a school in Athens: and surely we may take it for certain that he did do so, at least in the sense that he lectured to pupils regularly in an appointed place. There is no reason indeed to think that he lived with his pupils: but that feature in the *Clouds* is due to the superimposing of an Orphic community-life on to the school of Ionian science.

I have said that I see no reason to doubt that Socrates in his youth attended the lectures of Archelaus, the successor of Anaxagoras at Athens. This need not imply anything in the nature of original research by Socrates: it was natural that he should feel some interest in, and desire to acquaint himself with, the scientific opinions of his day; it is quite likely that he started with the eager enthusiasm which Plato attributes to him in the famous autobiographical

passage of the *Phaedo*[1] (96 A ff.). But he soon
found his studies unsatisfying: and if it be true,
as one account says,[2] that he spent several years
with Archelaus, it is probable that what kept
him was his teacher's lectures on ethics and
politics.[3]

It seems to me that it is only on these lines
that we can interpret the well-attested connexion
of Socrates with Archelaus consistently with the
evidence of the *Apology*. For that evidence rules
out anything beyond what we should nowadays
call an undergraduate course of study: it rules

[1] I do not imply that I accept this account as an
accurate statement of Socrates' intellectual develop-
ment. One reason for my inability to do so is that
it seems most unlikely that Socrates should have
become acquainted with the doctrine of Anaxagoras
in the accidental fashion described, and only *after* he
had given considerable attention to the doctrines of
other scientists. It was likely to be the first doctrine
he would come across, since Anaxagoras had taught
in Athens, and Archelaus had maintained, though
with some modification, his master's doctrine.

[2] Porphyry, *Hist. Philos.* fr. 12 (Diels, *Frag.
Vors.* I, p. 411).

[3] Diog. Laert. II, 16, ἔοικεν δὲ καὶ οὗτος ἅψασθαι τῆς
ἠθικῆς. καὶ γὰρ περὶ νόμων πεφιλοσόφηκε καὶ καλῶν καὶ
δικαίων· παρ' οὗ λαβὼν Σωκράτης τῷ αὐξῆσαι εἰς τὸ ⟨ἄκρον⟩
εὑρεῖν ὑπελήφθη.

out any independent advance upon or modification of teaching received: above all it rules out
the activity of a teacher of science (ἐγὼ δὲ διδάσκαλος μὲν οὐδενὸς πώποτ' ἐγενόμην, 33 A), and
the communication of an esoteric doctrine (εἰ
δέ τίς φησι παρ' ἐμοῦ πώποτέ τι μαθεῖν ἢ ἀκοῦσαι
ἰδίᾳ ὅτι μὴ καὶ οἱ ἄλλοι πάντες, εὖ ἴστε ὅτι οὐκ
ἀληθῆ λέγει, 33 B). πώποτε, be it observed, in
both places: not 'during the last 24 years'. It
may be said perhaps that Plato, who wrote the
word, was only thinking of the latter part of
Socrates' life, the years when he had known him.
That might pass if these passages stood by themselves: but standing as they do in connexion with
Socrates' detailed repudiation of the accounts
which made him out to be a teacher, an expounder
of scientific doctrines, they must surely be taken
at their face value.

Hence it was not because he was already
famous as a man of science that Chaerephon put
his question about Socrates to the Delphic oracle,
'Is there any man wiser than Socrates?' Why
then was it? This is not an easy question to
answer, but we can clear the ground by eliminat-
ing one recent theory, that of Horneffer,[1] which
at first sight looks plausible. Horneffer thinks

[1] *Op. cit.* pp. 76 ff. But, as will appear, Horneffer
gives a clue to what I think is the right solution.

that at the date of the *Clouds* (423 B.C.) Socrates had not yet come forward as a 'prover of men', that he was not yet the familiar figure that accosted everybody in the street and the market-place to reason of wisdom and right conduct: his activity was as yet private, confined to a circle of intimates. This is impossible if we accept (and Horneffer himself does absolutely accept) the evidence of the *Apology*. For according to the *Apology*, the popular misrepresentations which found dramatic exposition in the *Clouds* (and the *Connus* of Ameipsias) were the result of the irritation caused by Socrates' public activity: they originated with the victims of his cross-examination and that of his young imitators.

Hence it was before 423 that Socrates began fulfilling his divine mission: and although I should be chary of relying as confidently as Burnet[1] does on *Charmides*, 153 A (where Socrates is spoken of as resuming his mission after his return from Potidaea in 432–431) it is quite possible that he had begun it even before the Peloponnesian War broke out. Anyhow the oracle, if it was in fact the stimulus to his characteristic activity, was given some years before 423. But here a problem arises. Why is it that, as Horneffer points out, there is not a trace in

[1] *Greek Philosophy*, Part I, p. 136.

the *Clouds* of the Socrates who buttonholes the chance-comer in the street? Why is he rather represented (ll. 362–3) as the stage 'professor' who walks about oblivious of his fellow-creatures, with his eyes fixed on the clouds? I can see only one solution, namely that there was a break in Socrates' public activity,[1] partly no doubt caused by absence on military service (he was in the Delium campaign the year before the *Clouds*, just at the time when Aristophanes must have been writing the play), partly perhaps by a doubt whether his 'elenchtic' procedure of exposing the false conceit of wisdom might not be doing more harm than good just because it did arouse prejudice against him. I suggest that there was a period, about 435–431, during which he behaved as described in *Apology*, 21 B–23 B, going about accosting statesmen, poets, etc., followed by a period of private intercourse with those who had got to know about him, and also interrupted by military service. It was his quasi-retirement during the years 431–424 approximately that would enable the διαβολαί to flourish and fix themselves in Aristophanes' mind. Socrates con-

---

[1] Burnet (*op. cit.* p. 137) suggests that his mission was interrupted by the war, but does not contemplate the distinction here suggested between its public and private aspects.

sorted with his intimates in his own house, his thinking-shop, in those years. Later, perhaps after the Peace of Nicias, his public appearances were resumed and carried on to the end of his life. To come back to the question of Chaerephon's approaching the oracle, I suggest that the reputation for σοφία which it presupposes was due to an *earlier* period of private activity: though how early this started we cannot tell. Hence we get this scheme, which seems to fit the facts and the evidence: (1) from perhaps 450 to 435 Socrates, having abandoned his short-lived scientific interests, addresses himself to awakening a sense of spiritual values in a small circle of friends, who include Chaerephon, and who are deeply impressed with his insight into the fundamental questions of human life; (2) from the time of the oracle, perhaps 435, to 431 Socrates turns to a more public activity, an examination of the reputed wise men of Athens; an activity perhaps predominantly 'elenchtic' but certainly not wholly exclusive of positive content and moral guidance; (3) about 431–424 he reverts to the private activity of the first period, with frequent intervals of military service; (4) about 421 he returns to the conduct of the second period, but with a wider scope and probably more positive moral teaching: this continues down to 399. This scheme, in which the dates cannot of course be more than approximately correct, satisfies the two essential conditions: it allows the ἔλεγχος or ἐξέτασις of all and sundry to be due to, and immediately consequent on, the oracle to Chaerephon, and it admits a period during which Socrates acted in such a way as to win that reputation for 'wisdom' amongst his friends which the putting of Chaerephon's question pre-supposes, without attributing to him activities and interests which the whole tenour of the *Apology* rules out. It also helps us, I think, to understand why it is primarily the 'destructive' side of Socrates, the exposure of sham wisdom, that is, in the *Apology*, directly connected with the oracle. The scheme depends, of course, on our accepting what I have already argued, that the oracle was not in fact the sole *fons et origo* of Socrates' activity, of his pursuance of his divine mission.

I turn now to a consideration of the *Apology* in relation to that passage of the *Phaedo* which has already been incidentally noticed; and I shall necessarily be concerned chiefly with Burnet's interpretation of that dialogue.

In the lengthy introduction to his edition of the *Phaedo* Burnet deals most inadequately with the evidence of the *Apology* as to Socrates' scientific pursuits. The only references to that evidence are (1) p. xxxv footnote, where it is remarked that 'The references to Aristophanes in the *Apology* are little more than Socratic *persiflage*', and (2) p. xlii, where it is said that 'It is quite natural that Socrates should be classed with those who busy themselves with "things aloft" (τὰ μετέωρα), but we regularly find that "the things beneath the earth" (τὰ ὑπὸ γῆς) are associated with these in his case': to this sentence there is a footnote, 'Cp. *Apol.* 18 B 7, τά τε μετέωρα φροντιστὴς καὶ τὰ ὑπὸ γῆς πάντα ἀνεζητηκώς, *Clouds* 188, ζητοῦσιν οὗτοι τὰ κατὰ γῆς'. There is not a hint given that the description of Socrates in *Apology*, 18 B 7, is said there by Socrates himself to be sheer misrepresentation: and anyone who read this Introduction without knowing the *Apology* would naturally draw the inference that the *Apology* supports the evidence of this line quoted from the *Clouds*.

In the same author's *Greek Philosophy*, Part I, § 112, where he turns to consider how far the Platonic account of Socrates 'is confirmed or otherwise by Aristophanes' he starts out by saying, 'In the first place, we must observe that Plato represents the life of Sokrates as sharply divided into two periods by the response of the oracle'. But where does he do so? The *Apology* is the only work in which Plato mentions this oracle, and he does not there represent it as sharply dividing Socrates' life into two periods: for to do so he must have told us something about the earlier period, while in fact he tells us nothing about it. Burnet's next sentence would lead the ordinary reader to suppose that Socrates described this earlier period (by reference to the activities which characterised it) in connexion with his mention of the oracle and the oracle's effect, viz. the pursuit of the 'divine mission': the sentence runs thus—'In the earlier, he was chiefly occupied with the religious and scientific movements of his time, and with his new theory of the participation of sensible things in the "forms"; in the latter, his mission to his fellow-citizens is his chief, and almost his sole interest...'. This is not a summary of what we are told *either* in the *Apology or* in the *Phaedo*, but a fusion of the two accounts which is illegitimate for this reason, that each taken by itself is not complementary to the other, but contradictory of the other. The *Apology* knows nothing of a 'pre-mission' pursuit of science or of the theory of Forms, the *Phaedo* knows nothing of a 'post-theory-of-Forms' mission; and both ac-

counts have all the appearance of giving, or
meaning to give, a *complete* account of Socrates'
interests and pursuits. If we had had the two
accounts without the name of Socrates attached
to them, would anybody have guessed that they
referred to one and the same man? Further, in
case there be anyone who imagines that my
argument is merely *ex silentio* (or *ex silentiis*), I
will call his attention once more to the sentence
at *Apology*, 19 D, with its πώποτε: ἀξιῶ ὑμᾶς
ἀλλήλους διδάσκειν τε καὶ φράζειν, ὅσοι ἐμοῦ
πώποτε ἀκηκόατε διαλεγομένου—πολλοὶ δὲ ὑμῶν
οἱ τοιοῦτοί εἰσιν—φράζετε οὖν ἀλλήλοις εἰ πώποτε
ἢ μικρὸν ἢ μέγα ἤκουσέ τις ὑμῶν ἐμοῦ περὶ τῶν
τοιούτων διαλεγομένου, and I will ask him to set
beside it as a complement *Phaedo*, 100 A–B,
especially ἀλλ᾽, ἦ δ᾽ ὅς, ὧδε λέγω, οὐδὲν καινόν, ἀλλ᾽
ἅπερ ἀεί τε ἄλλοτε καὶ ἐν τῷ παρεληλυθότι λόγῳ
οὐδὲν πέπαυμαι λέγων. ἔρχομαι γὰρ δὴ ἐπιχειρῶν
σοι ἐνδείξασθαι τῆς αἰτίας τὸ εἶδος ὃ πεπραγ-
μάτευμαι, καὶ εἶμι πάλιν ἐπ᾽ ἐκεῖνα τὰ πολυθρύλητα
καὶ ἄρχομαι ἀπ᾽ ἐκείνων, ὑποθέμενος εἶναί τι καλὸν
αὐτὸ καθ᾽ αὑτὸ καὶ ἀγαθὸν καὶ μέγα καὶ τἆλλα
πάντα. *This* Socrates has always been busying
himself with a metaphysical theory—he has talked
so much about it that it has become πολυθρύλητον,
a hackneyed theme. But, on the theory we are

discussing, it had lost interest and importance
for Socrates, who since 435 or so had concerned himself, as 'his chief, and almost his sole
interest', with his mission to his fellow-citizens.

Let us however, for the sake of argument,
waive this difficulty. Let us suppose that Socrates the gadfly, and the philosopher who was
always talking about his Forms, co-existed simul-
taneously in the later years of the fifth century.
To whom did he impart, with whom did he discuss, his doctrine? We shall be told that it was
with his ἑταῖροι, his special circle of intimates.
In that case he is at least somewhat inexact in
saying at *Apology*, 33 b, εἰ δέ τίς φησι παρ' ἐμοῦ
πώποτέ τι μαθεῖν ἢ ἀκοῦσαι ἰδίᾳ, ὅτι μὴ καὶ οἱ
ἄλλοι πάντες, εὖ ἴστε ὅτι οὐκ ἀληθῆ λέγει. But
let that pass: and I will ask, where is our
evidence for this circle of intimates, Aristophanes
being *ex hypothesi* excluded as a witness. In
Plato I have searched for them in vain: in *Greek
Philosophy*, Part I, they appear to be found (1) in a
sentence of the *Memorabilia* (I, 6, § 14) where
the word is, in point of fact, φίλοι: 'The treasures
that the wise men of old have left us in their
writings I open and explore with my friends';
and the context makes it plain that the treasures
in question were the moral teaching of the old
poets; (2) in the list of Σωκράτους ὁμιληταί at

Mem. I, 2, § 48, men who 'consorted with him, not that they might shine in the courts or the assembly, but that they might become καλοί τε κἀγαθοί, and be able to do their duty by house and household, relatives and friends, city and citizens'; (3) in the list at *Phaedo*, 59 B ff., of those present, and those whose absence needed comment, at the last scene in the prison. It is the last of these three passages alone that gives any colour to the suggestion of an intimate circle of friends sharing philosophical doctrine. Now that some of Socrates' friends were more intimate with him than others is only to be expected: and that it was they who came to the prison on the last day is again perfectly natural: but where is our warrant for supposing that they were ἑταῖροι in the sense of associates in a philosophical doctrine?[1]

Burnet finds it in the ready acceptance by

---

[1] Field, *Plato and his Contemporaries*, p. 152, says 'As far as we can judge, the Socrates of Aeschines even more than the Socrates of Xenophon is entirely occupied with problems of practical morality'. This is, I think, undeniable. Yet Aeschines was one of the friends present on the last day, and was famous in antiquity for the accuracy of his portraits of Socrates. Why then do we find in him no trace of a Socratic theory of Forms?

Socrates' interlocutors in this dialogue of the doctrine of Forms, whenever it is mentioned, and the familiarity with which they greet it. Now it is perfectly true that we find Simmias speaking in this way at 65 D, 74 B, and most emphatically at 77 A, where he says, οὐ γὰρ ἔχω ἔγωγε οὐδὲν οὕτω μοι ἐναργὲς ὂν ὡς τοῦτο, τὸ πάντα τὰ τοιαῦτ᾽ εἶναι ὡς οἷόν τε μάλιστα, καλόν τε καὶ ἀγαθὸν καὶ τἆλλα πάντα ἃ σὺ νυνδὴ ἔλεγες. But it is, in the first place, a considerable step from this attitude on the part of Simmias to the assertion that all the other persons present, because they do not interrupt or ask for explanations, share Simmias' belief. And secondly, the main object of the discussion is to show that the immortality of the soul can be inferred from the theory of Forms; that theory itself is, to Plato, an ἄμεσος καὶ ἀναπόδεικτος ἀρχή, a presupposition of all philosophical argument: hence if in a dialogue anything were to be inferred from it, Socrates was bound to have a respondent who admitted this premiss. I take it that to attribute to Simmias this familiarity with the theory is the natural and inevitable way for Plato to indicate that the theory is a first premiss which must be unquestionably postulated if anything is to be proved.

This explanation seems confirmed by a later

passage, 100 B. There, after Socrates has referred to the Forms as ἐκεῖνα τὰ πολυθρύλητα, he continues, 'If you grant me these and admit that they exist, I hope that I shall discover and prove to you the reason for the immortality of Soul'; and Cebes, who is now the respondent, replies, 'Well, take it that I do grant that, and proceed with all haste'. If Cebes had, as a matter of historical fact, been associated as a ἑταῖρος with Socrates in Burnet's sense and with his implications, Socrates would not have addressed him in this tentative fashion, nor would Plato have represented him as doing so.

Moreover we find very much the same procedure at *Republic*, 596 A, where Socrates says to Glaucon, 'Would you like to start our enquiry with the customary procedure? We are accustomed, I think, to postulate a single unity in connexion with each plurality of things to which we apply the same name' (βούλει οὖν ἐνθένδε ἀρξώμεθα ἐπισκοποῦντες, ἐκ τῆς εἰωθυίας μεθόδου; εἶδος γάρ πού τι ἓν ἕκαστον εἰώθαμεν τίθεσθαι περὶ ἕκαστα τὰ πολλὰ οἷς ταὐτὸν ὄνομα ἐπιφέρομεν). Here we have the first person plural, which Burnet finds so significant in the *Phaedo*, and although Glaucon has not the exuberant enthusiasm of Simmias, we have the same assumption of a shared doctrine. Glaucon too should qualify for membership of the inner circle.[1]

Why are Simmias and Cebes chosen as respondents or interlocutors in the *Phaedo*? Surely because Plato knew that his theory of Forms has affinities with the Pythagorean Number-doctrine, and the assent to that theory, which was vital for the main theses of the dialogue, might with the best dramatic plausibility be expressed by persons who knew something of Pythagoreanism. Not that I doubt that they were in fact intimate friends of Socrates. Cebes was a friend of Plato also (Plato, *Epistle* XIII, 363 A), a fact which is perhaps not without significance: it may well be that he, and perhaps Simmias too, really held the Theory of Forms that Plato formulated.

My conclusion then is that the *Phaedo* cannot legitimately be used any more than the *Clouds* to discredit, to modify, or to supplement the evidence of the *Apology*, save in so far as it may give a roughly correct account of Socrates' early scientific interests.

[1] As indeed he does in Taylor, *Varia Socratica*, p. 144. But of the numerous passages in the *Republic* which disprove this notion I am content to quote 608 D: οὐκ ᾔσθησαι, ἦν δ' ἐγώ, ὅτι ἀθάνατος ἡμῶν ἡ ψυχὴ καὶ οὐδέποτε ἀπόλλυται; καὶ ὃς ἐμβλέψας μοι καὶ θαυμάσας εἶπε, Μὰ Δί', οὐκ ἔγωγε· σὺ δὲ τοῦτ' ἔχεις λέγειν;

ADDITIONAL NOTES

(1) While this book was in the Press, Professor A. E. Taylor's *Socrates* (Peter Davies, 1932) was published, and I think it desirable to mention some points in which I find it impossible to agree with his views.

Professor Taylor recognises (p. 19) a marked contrast between the Socrates of the 'thinking-shop' and the 'Platonic (or Xenophontic) Socrates with his mission to everyone who will listen to him'; and suggests that 'when we remember that Aristophanes is burlesquing Socrates as he was, or was believed to be, at a time when Plato and Xenophon were little more than babies, we should see that the contrast may well be largely explained by this difference in date. It may prove to be the fact that Socrates at forty-five was in some ways a different man from Socrates at fifty-five or sixty...'.

This disregards the fact that the Socrates with the mission, who is so unlike the Socrates of the *Clouds*, is the Socrates who describes himself, and emphasises the falsity of the Aristophanic picture, in the *Apology*. If Socrates did in fact repudiate that picture, as Professor Taylor would apparently allow since 'we may be con-

fident that Plato's version' of Socrates' speech
in his defence 'has reproduced it with close
accuracy' (p. 116), there surely is the most
decisive evidence we could wish that that picture
is completely false. If, on the other hand, the
repudiation of the picture is fathered upon
Socrates by Plato, then we have got to choose
between Plato's belief about what Socrates'
interests were in his early life and Aristophanes'
completely contradictory account: for myself
I should not hesitate long over my choice.
Moreover, Professor Taylor's contention that
the Platonic Socrates is the Socrates of later life
ignores the probability (which, however, he
recognises in the footnote to p. 62) that Plato
would have taken the trouble to find out something about his master's earlier life and interests,
particularly if he were undertaking to publish
such an account of Socrates' life as he did (on this
second supposition) in the *Apology*. But indeed
I find it difficult to discover in Professor Taylor's
book any clear and consistent view as to the
nature of the evidence furnished by the *Apology*.
For how can the words I have just quoted from
p. 116 be reconciled with the following passages
(where the italics are mine)?—

'*Plato makes a point of it* that his poverty was
directly due to absorption in a mission which

left no time for attendance to "personal affairs".'
(p. 40.)

'Plato makes it quite clear that *in his own belief* Chaerephon's question was put to the oracle before the outbreak of the Peloponnesian War.... For Socrates *is made in the Apology* to account for his popularity....' (p. 78.)

'Since, as we see from the *Apology*, reminiscences of the *Clouds* were *held by Plato* to have helped to secure the condemnation of Socrates....' (p. 86.)

On p. 67 Professor Taylor writes: 'Perhaps we may even conjecture that when Archelaus died...Socrates was to all intents and purposes his successor. This may sound startling to us when we remember the vigour with which the Socrates of Plato's *Apology* denies that he has any "disciples" or has ever professed to be any man's teacher, but it is strictly consistent with the denials of Plato. What Socrates is concerned to deny in the *Apology* is that he has ever followed the profession of a paid "educator of men" or taken "pupils". This is quite compatible with his having at some time before Plato's own birth been the unpaid head of a body of "associates" over whose studies he had presided'.

In the first place, I do not understand why the

fall roughly rather more than twenty years before Plato's own birth, the picture is, of course,
an imaginative reconstruction, but there were
plenty of members of Plato's own family circle
from whom he could derive the necessary information'. Similarly on p. 167 he regards these
pages of the *Parmenides* as good evidence of the
way in which Socrates was led to his doctrine of
Forms. Now on p. 172 Professor Taylor allows
that it is 'Plato himself' who in the *Parmenides*
points out incisively the difficulties inherent in
the doctrine: that is to say, the objections are
not those of Parmenides, but Parmenides is a
mouthpiece of Plato. What reason have we to
regard the picture of Socrates in that dialogue as
more historical than that of Parmenides? Or
why should we suppose, as presumably we must
if 'Parmenides' = Plato, that the perplexity to
which Socrates is reduced at 133 A and 135 C is
a projection of Plato's own perplexity, and yet
that the exposition of doctrine leading to that
perplexity is Socrates' own?

(2) p. 31 (bottom) 'natural conclusion'. The
μέν in the sentence quoted is not answered by
the δέ in κατὰ τοὺς νόμους δέ κτλ. It is *solitarium*:
cf. similar concluding formulae in *Mem.* I, iv, 19
and I, vii, 5.

(3) p. 42 (top) 'an early work of Xenophon's'. I should add that the opening words Σωκράτους δὲ ἄξιον κτλ. cannot imply that the work was originally appended to *Mem.*: they could only show that it was appended to an account of somebody other than Socrates. The δέ must have been added by an editor or copyist who thought that the work belonged to *Mem.* (So von Arnim, *op. cit.*, p. 54.)

INDEX

CAMBRIDGE: PRINTED BY
W. LEWIS, M.A.
AT THE UNIVERSITY PRESS